Humanity, Our Place in the Universe

The Central Beliefs

of

The World's Major Religions

Colin Drake

Copyright © 2011 by Colin Drake

First Edition

All rights reserved. No part of this book shall be reproduced or transmitted, for commercial purposes, without written permission from the author.

Published by Colin Drake

ISBN: 978-0-9871655-1-0

Cover design by the author.

Also by the same author:

A Light Unto Your Self

Self Discovery
Through
Investigation of Experience

Beyond The Separate Self
The End of Anxiety and Mental Suffering

Poetry
From
Beyond The Separate Self

These titles are available as: e-books, hard cover and paperbacks from
www.lulu.com/spotlight/colin108atbigponddotc

Contents

Introduction	4
1. Judaism	10
2. Christianity	23
3. Islam	35
4. Hinduism	48
5. Buddhism	62
6. Ramakrishna: A Living Example	77
7. Comparison and Conclusion	110
Glossary	119
Bibliography	124
Index	130

Introduction

This book considers the place of humanity in the universe according to the world's major religions: Judaism, Christianity, Islam, Hinduism and Buddhism. This is accomplished by exploring the correlation between self-identity and world-view in each of these in turn; that is to say, the interaction between the way in which adherents of a particular religious viewpoint see, or define, themselves and the way in which they see and relate to the world. This exploration requires examining the central beliefs of these religions, for it is within the framework of these beliefs that the concepts of self-identity and world-view become apparent. There are many different forms of self-identity, examples being materialist, dualist, monist, universal and even that of no-self (*anatta*) in Buddhism. These inform and are informed by one's view of the world and one's place in it, and a change in either, by religious conversion for example, may radically change the other.

This analysis highlights the similarities and differences of the place and function of the individual in the world's five major religions: Judaism, Christianity, Islam, Hinduism and Buddhism. It also shows why some religions stress participation in the world and human affairs, whereas others are more focussed on the personal journey towards enlightenment and considers the relationship between self-identity and the belief, or lack of belief, in the afterlife. The world-view of each religion helps explain the different lifestyles adopted by its adherents, some seemingly centred on material acquisition and enjoyment, others on being 'good' so as to gain entry to heaven, others on devoting oneself or submitting to a chosen deity and finally the path of detachment and spiritual practices to attain enlightenment.

The world-view to be considered is the purely religious view of an adherent to a particular religious system and not the political, legalistic, or cultural view which may be imposed by the authorities of this system in different parts of the world. This religious view should be common to adherents of each system worldwide and is primary to the shaping of a sincere follower's world-view, whereas the local political, legalistic and cultural mores of that system are variable and should be of secondary importance in the formation of a devotee's view of the world. The laws, rules, rituals and practices specified in the system's scriptures are part of the framework in which an adherent can achieve life's purpose, as specified by that system, but are not to be considered here, as this part of the framework lies outside the scope of this book.

In order to study this religious view, I will consider five elements, that is to say, the way that religious systems answer the five big existential questions:

1. **God:** Is there a God, or an Absolute and if so what is its nature?

2. **Creation**: How was the universe created and what is the nature and purpose of this creation?

3. **The Nature of Man**: What is the essential nature of a human being – are we ephemeral material beings or do we possess some kind of indestructible essence?

4. **The Purpose of Life:** What is the purpose of life?

5. **The Afterlife**: What happens upon the death of the human body? Does this entail annihilation or is there some kind of afterlife and, if so, what is its nature?

As can be clearly seen, the world-view based on the answers to these questions contain the notion of self-identity such that a sudden change of one's conception of self-identity by a religious experience or sudden conversion will lead to a significant change of one's world-view.

In each religion is presented the orthodox or fundamental view, based entirely on that religion's scriptures, and at least one other view that has developed since these scriptures were written down. However, this book does not consider how or when these developments came about, for it is the present day view of the world and self-identity within these religious systems that is being studied. For instance, if you are a Catholic and thus believe that you possess (are in fact) an immortal soul, this is what is important to you, and not how this idea developed from the interaction between early Christianity and Hellenistic philosophy. This brings up an important point: what is being studied is the interaction between world-view and self-identity in the religious system itself, and therefore only applies to someone who accepts and believes what that system says. A once a week 'Sunday' Catholic, or a sceptic born into Catholicism who uses it as an 'insurance policy', may find that her life is only marginally influenced by the Catholic world-view.

It is already becoming clear that discovering the answers to these five questions and thus the religious world-view within any religious system can only be done by studying that system from the inside out. That is to say, finding out what that system itself says and believes, either by studying the scriptures themselves with informed comment from those within that system, or by studying the writings and teachings of prominent leaders and commentators within the system. External commentators can be useful only where they are entirely sympathetic to the system in question and are thus unlikely to distort the views of that system based on their own views and prejudices. To ameliorate the effects of my personal bias, I have attempted to adopt an empathetic approach to each system studied.

The book is divided into five chapters, one on each of the religions being studied. In the Western tradition, Judaism is considered first, then Christianity and finally Islam, as they developed in that order, the latter two with the preceding religion(s) and their scripture(s) as a base. With regard to the Eastern religions, Hinduism is considered first, as the older Upanishads predate the birth of Buddha.[1]

The following scriptures are the primary sources used extensively in the sections on Judaism, Christianity, Islam and Hinduism: The Bible, The Qur'an, The Upanishads and The Bhagavad Gita. When the first three are quoted, two translations were checked against each other, and where there were substantial differences the alternate translation

---

[1] P. Williams, *Buddhist Thought*, 2000, London, p.12

is provided in brackets. In the section on Gaudiya Vaishnavism, all quotes from the Bhagavad Gita are from the translation by A.C.Bhaktivedanta Swami Prabhupada, who is the foremost authority of this sect of Vaishnavism. In this case no other source was used as it is the world-view of this stream of Vaishnavism which is being studied. In all of the above cases each quote is not individually footnoted, but the chapter and verse numbers are provided and the translations of the scriptures used are given in the bibliography. In the section on Buddhism all quotes are individually referenced as there is no single major scriptural source.

With regard to secondary sources, I relied on experts from within each system being studied, for these are the ones that enunciate the world-view of that system without any external interpretation. This means that books by, and websites of, such people as rabbis, theologians, priests, imams, Sufi masters, Swamis, gurus, Buddhist monks and Tibetan lamas, were all useful. External commentators were only accessed where they either quote such sources or where the writer is either a follower of, or obviously sympathetic to, the system in question.

Each chapter considers the five elements, that is, answers the big questions of world-view, from the scriptural and a later viewpoint. Within this enunciation of the world-view the concept of self-identity of the religious adherent becomes clear. These elements are studied in the same order within each religion: God, creation, man's nature, the purpose of life and the afterlife. There is then an analysis of the correlation between this view of self-identity and each of the elements within the world-view to show how they interact with and help form each other.

Next there is a chapter on Sri Ramakrishna as an example of the themes discussed. He was chosen as he followed many of these different paths, achieving the final goal of each one. He is the only person I am aware of who accomplished this and his views can be considered with reference to both Hindu paths considered, plus those of Christianity and Islam. Finally there is a chapter which sums up and shows the similarities and differences between the religions discussed.

Chapter One
Judaism

In Judaism consideration is given to the orthodox scriptural view and that of Kabbalah, literally 'received' wisdom, which is a mystical path based on a number of Aramaic texts from the late 13th century, which together constitute the Zohar. These were probably composed by the Spanish mystic Moses de Leon, who maintained that they were based on the writings of a famous rabbi from the second century C.E., Simeon bar Yohai.[2]

God

Firstly, considering the nature or attributes of God in the Judaic scripture, the Tanakh or Old Testament, God is described as: 'One' (Deuteronomy 6 v.4), but also as the 'God of Gods' (Ibid 10 v.17 and Daniel 2 v.47) and 'greater than all Gods' (Chronicles 2 v.5). This tends to indicate a belief in a multitude of gods, of whom God is the greatest.

'Eternal' (Job 36 v.26 and Isaiah 57 v.15), 'The ruler of heaven' (Deuteronomy 10 v.14), 'All knowing' (2 Samuel 14 v.20), 'Holy' (Psalms 99 v.9 and others) and 'In heaven' as compared to 'on earth' (Ecclesiastes 5 v.2). These references highlight the transcendental, omniscient, omnipotent nature of the Absolute.

---

[2] Carl S. Erlich, *Understanding Judaism*, London, 2004, p. 47.

He is 'the Creator of heaven and earth' (Genesis Chapter 1), 'The King of all the earth' (Psalms 47 v.7) and the 'giver' of the Promised Land to the Israelites (Deuteronomy 19 v.1-3 and many more). Thus He is the creator and ruler of the earth and has singled out the Israelites as a 'chosen race' by 'giving' them the Promised Land.

Also He is 'with you' (Joshua 1 v.9, Isaiah 8 v.8-10 and many more), 'Walking among you' (Deuteronomy 23 v.14) and in Job 27 v.3 it says: 'The spirit (breath) of God is my life.' These references point to the immanence of the Absolute who is always present.

He is not only present but 'Our safe place (refuge)' (Psalms 62 v.8), 'my helper' (Isaiah 50 v.7), 'their strength' (Job 12 v.13 and many more), our 'protector' (Proverbs 30 v.5), 'teacher' (Isaiah 28 v.26) and 'salvation' (Jeremiah 3 v.23 and Psalms 68 v.20). Thus not only is He immanent, but He also intervenes to help and protect us, if we deserve it. As well as helping man, He also is a 'judge, angry with evil-doers; (Psalms 7 v.11 and 75 v.7) whilst at the same time He is 'upright (righteous)' (Daniel 9 v.14) and 'full of grace and mercy' (2 Chronicles 30 v.9).

There is some debate as to whether He was thought to be anthropomorphic for whilst it says in Genesis 1 v.27 that He 'created man in his own image', it also says that He 'is not a man or the son of a man' (Numbers 23 v.19). It would appear that while this does not mean that He is anthropomorphic, in form, it was used to highlight man's special status above that of all other created beings. This also 'emphasises the continuity of God's being with man's being, projecting God as a more powerful, more moral man-like entity. God emerges as personal, caring about man and needing to be placated by man'.[3] So whilst the Absolute is transcendent, omnipotent, omniscient and eternal, He is also immanent and intervenes to help or punish us as we deserve. Not only that but He is personal with a superman-like nature with whom we can and should build a personal relationship.

The Kabbalistic Zohar attempts to grasp the mystery of God by the development of a complex system to categorize the different levels of the Godhead.[4] In this system the source of creation, the ultimate infinite Godhead about which nothing can be said, is called Ein-Sof. Out of this came light, followed by the creation (Genesis 1 v.1-41) which the Kabbalists regard as the vessel that receives the light and it is this interaction between the vessel and the light that keeps the universe functioning.[5]

Creation

Creation itself is based on ten basic elements, the Sefirot, which come from the ten uses of *va-omerelohim* ('and God {Elohim} said') in the opening chapter of the Torah. These represent the manifest attributes of the divine and are usually noted as kingdom, wisdom, understanding, loving-kindness, strength, beauty, triumph/dominance, grandeur/empathy, foundation and sovereignty. Together they

---

[3] A. Unterman, *The Jews*, 1981, Boston, p. 20.
[4] Carl S. Erlich, *Understanding Judaism*, London, 2004, p. 47.
[5] Rabbi David A. Cooper, *God is a Verb*, New York, 1997, p. 76.

constitute the Kabbalistic Tree of Life, the essential foundation of all creation.[6]

The universe was created, according to the Torah (the first five books of the Tanakh), out of the mind of and by the word of God. For example 'God said "let there be light" and there was light' (Genesis 1. v.3), and 'God said, "Let the earth give birth to all sorts of living things, cattle and all things moving on the earth and beasts of the earth after their sort": and it was so.' (Genesis 1 v.24). Thus the universe came into being purely by the thought and command of God who rested after His creation and was pleased with the results: 'and God saw all that He had made and it was very good' (Genesis 1 v.31). It appears that God made the universe because it pleased Him to do so and for His enjoyment. This concept is supported in the Talmud, the Jewish book of law, which states that 'every person will have to give an accounting for all the good things created on earth that he, or she, denied himself, or herself, from enjoying'.[7] Men and women, who are made in 'God's image' (Genesis 1 v.27), are enjoined to participate and take pleasure in God's creation. As Rabbi Benjamin Blech says: 'God decorated His house so magnificently that Judaism believes He takes it personally if you don't share His excitement and joy in everything He has put on this earth'.[8]

Kabbalah puts a slightly different emphasis on this by saying that human consciousness, being 'made in the image of God', is not only a

---

[6] *Ibid* p.83-84.
[7] Rabbi Benjamin Blech, *Understanding Judaism*, Indianapolis, 1999, p. 56.
[8] *Ibid,* p.56.

vessel for receiving the light, as is everything in manifestation, but also has the capacity to bestow the light. That is to say, humans are capable of both enjoying and continuing God's creation. According to Rabbi David Cooper, 'This human capacity of acting like God in being a bestower is the fulcrum on which the entire universe is balanced'.[9] The implications of this are that creation is an unfinished business which is influenced by the actions of humanity, especially in the use of free will in giving and creating.

The Nature of Man

Human beings 'made in the image of God' potentially have the same attributes as God in terms of creativity, bestowing and enjoying. However, how do Biblical Judaism and Kabbalah define self-identity, the essential nature of a person? In this investigation only the Torah will be considered as this constitutes the 'primary religious text of Judaism'[10], about which 'the primary orthodox opinion is that God dictated these [chapters] to Moses who wrote them down in the forms we read today'.[11] In this, man is seen as a material creature which is animated by God's breath, or life-force: 'and the Lord God made man from the dust of the earth, breathing into him the breath of life; and man became a living soul' (Genesis 2 v.7). This 'breath' is not confined to man but animates all living beings: 'they went with Noah into the ark, two and two of all flesh in which is the breath of life' (Genesis 7 v.15). The word 'soul' does not represent a separate individual dualistic entity

---

[9] Rabbi David A Cooper, *God is a Verb*, New York, 1997, p. 76-77.
[10] Carl S. Erlich, *Understanding Judaism*, London, 2004, p. 38.
[11] Rabbi Michael Levin, *Jewish Spirituality and Mysticism*, Indianapolis, 2002, p. 22.

in the Cartesian sense but simply means a living being, for it is made quite clear that 'from dust you are and to the dust you will go back.' (Genesis 3 v.19). All of the occurrences of the word 'soul' in the King James version of the Bible are simply translated as 'men' or 'people' in the later New English Bible and Bible in Basic English, except from those in Deuteronomy where there are numerous references to 'with all of your heart and with all of your soul'. These refer to the understanding that one is to love or turn to God with the totality of one's being. A person is a material being animated by the 'breath of God' (life-force) and upon death the person returns to the material elements from which they came, whilst the life-force returns to God. As Eliezer Segal says, 'The authors of the Hebrew Bible did not teach that man survives death in any religiously significant way'.[12]

However, many centuries later the Kabbalists had developed the idea of a soul that transmigrates from birth to birth and realm to realm until it finally returns to its source, the Ein-Sof. Each human was seen as an individual microcosm modelled on the Sefirot which reflected the nature of the cosmos, and was essentially a soul housed in an ephemeral corporeal body. This soul had to achieve purity and perfection on its journey through physical lives and higher realms until it could 'return to the infinite from which it emanated'.[13] Thus self-identity is equated with a separate incorporeal soul which travels from body to body and realm to realm. This may initially seem to be Cartesian dualism, but it is essentially monistic in that the soul

---

[12] Eliezer Segal, *Judaism*, in 'Life After Death in World Religions', ed. Harold Coward, New York, 1997, p.13.
[13] Dan Cohn-Sherbrook, *Jewish Mysticism*, Oxford, 1995, p.28-30.

emanates from the Ein-Sof, as does everything, and eventually returns back into this.

The Purpose of Life

However, for orthodox biblical Judaism, 'The aim of Jewish life is not the hereafter but fulfilment for individuals and communities through adherence to the laws of life.'[14] This fulfilment is to be gained from enjoying life, loving and helping others and being creative in the world. Leviticus 19 v.18 states that you should 'not make attempts to get equal with one who has done you wrong, or keep hard feelings against the children of your people, but have love for your neighbour as for yourself'; and Genesis 2 v.3 states that 'God blessed the seventh day and made it holy, because on that day he ceased from all the work he had set himself to do'. Jewish commentators read this to mean that God left creation unfinished so that man could serve as 'a partner to God in the act of creation.'[15] This partnership is bound by the covenant between God and Israel and delineated in the Torah in which God promised to deliver the Israelites from bondage and lead them to the Promised Land, in return for which they agreed to follow His divine commandments. God is also obliged to care for those who obey Him and it is within this structure that individuals can achieve fulfilment.[16]

---

[14] Professor Leen E. Goodman, *Jewish Philosophy*, in 'The Oxford Companion to Philosophy', Oxford, 2005, p.460.
[15] Rabbi David A Cooper, *God is a Verb*, New York, 1997, p.30.
[16] Carl S. Erlich, *Understanding Judaism*, London, 2004, p. 26.

Kabbalah agrees with the aims of creating, enjoying and helping others, but puts these within the framework of achieving spiritual transformation. This is to be achieved by transforming the desire to 'receive the light' into the desire to share this light with others. This bestowing of the light is not only about sharing but also to do with creatively changing the world for the better by transforming our own nature and assisting others to do likewise.[17] This perfecting of one's nature is the aim of life and 'indeed Judaism says that the very purpose of existence is the continuous perfecting of the universe.'[18]

The Afterlife

Kabbalists maintain that this process of purification and achieving perfection is necessary for the soul to finally break out of the cycle of transmigration and eventually return to God. However, there is no hint of this in the Torah which states that man is composed of and returns to dust. As for heaven, where this word occurs in the Torah it can be equated to 'the heavens' or the sky/firmament; and 'the underworld' (in the Basic English Bible) is translated as 'grave' (in the St James Bible) or 'pit' (in the New English Bible). There are also passages in the Torah which warn of the dire consequences of disobeying God's laws, but these are always couched in worldly terms such as plagues, fevers, defeats, famines, desolation and exile. Nowhere are these couched in terms of any after-worldly fate awaiting such 'sinners'.[19] It is true that

---

[17] Michael Berg, *The Way*, New York, 2001, p227-228.
[18] Rabbi David A Cooper, *God is a Verb*, New York, 1997, p. 77.
[19] Eliezer Segal, *Judaism*, in 'Life After Death in World Religions', ed. Harold Coward, New York, 1997, p.13.

later books of the Tanakh have passages that can be read to imply belief in the afterlife, but these could well be due to the influence of Hellenistic ideas in which the afterlife figured prominently. As Rabbi Michael Levin says:

> In the Torah there are no explicit references to a "world to come" nor are there any statements referring to an individual judging of souls... Intriguingly by the time you get to the Talmud, approximately 1800 years ago, you find that most of the words used to describe the afterlife come from the Greek ... Most Jews in the US – almost 85 per cent – belong to branches of Judaism which do not accept any sort of afterlife.[20]

In Ecclesiastes, a much later book than those of the Torah, it is quite explicitly stated that 'the fate of the sons of men and the fate of the beasts is the same ... All go to one place, all are of the dust and all will be turned to dust again.' (Ecclesiastes 3 v.19-20)

Analysis

Now an analysis of the correlation between the two concepts of self-identity and world-view enunciated. Each element of world-view (God, creation, man, purpose and the afterlife) is considered in relation to self-identity. Firstly, summing up the two views of self-identity, that of the Torah is primarily materialistic - that a person is purely a physical being (from dust) which is animated by a life-force (the 'breath' of God) and that this person ceases to be (to dust) when that life-force is withdrawn (the person dies). The Kabbalists have a monistic view that

---

[20] Rabbi Michael Levin, *Jewish Spirituality and Mysticism*, Indianapolis, 2002, p. 160.

everything emanates from and returns to the Ein-Sof, the infinite nothingness, but during manifestation the person has a basically dualistic nature. This consists of the body, which is physical and ephemeral, and the soul, which travels from body to body, and realm to realm, until it achieves perfection and purity when it will return back into the Ein-Sof.

Considering the first of these, a person is purely a material being which is animated by God and made in his image. This implies that man has potentially the same nature as God and this is borne out by the first acts of God, creation and enjoyment, which Jews believe are two of the purposes of human life. They also believe that they are His servants: 'For they are my servants whom I took out from the land of Egypt' (Leviticus 25 v.42) and thus they should follow God's commandments. Also, that God is believed to be immanent and omniscient implies that He experiences and acts in the world through us. As Abraham Joshua Herschel said:

> God is the centre towards which all forces tend. He is the source and we are the flowing of His force, the ebb and flow of His tides... For when we betake ourselves to the extreme opposite of the ego, we can behold a situation from the aspect of God.[21]
>
> Man is man because something divine is at stake in his existence. He is not an innocent bystander in the cosmic drama. There is in us more kinship with the divine than we are able to believe.[22]

---

[21] Abraham J. Herschel, *Man's Quest for God*, in 'God in all Worlds', ed. By Lucinda Vardey, Alexandria NSW, 1997, p.407
[22] *Ibid*, p.396.

Provided we remain aware of His presence and follow His will, we become instruments, or servants, through which He can carry out His dual purposes of creation and enjoyment. This is to be achieved by 'keep(ing) in mind the Lord Your God' (Deuteronomy 8 v.18 and others) and obeying His commandments. This brings us to the third purpose in life, which is to love and care for one's fellow man; for all humans are potentially instruments of God and should be respected and treated as such. We are also encouraged to be fruitful and multiply (Genesis 9 v.7) so as to create more potential instruments for God's purpose, and to avoid pride and vanity, for we come from and return to dust. So essentially a person is a material instrument or servant of God, animated by Him, and which ceases on death. If the person keeps his covenant with God and serves Him then God cares for that person. However, those persons who forget God and who disobey His commandments are of no service to Him and are liable to suffer dire consequences.

The Kabbalists have similar ideas but posit that the person, as an individual, comes from God and survives many transmigrations until returning to God. The person is essentially a material body containing a soul which is a vessel that receives light from the ultimate Godhead or Ein-Sof and can also bestow that light on others. In this way the soul is also an instrument of the divine in that it can act as a bestower of light, as does God. This bestowing of the light is achieved by caring for others, the other instruments, or vessels, of God, and enjoying the creation and creatively perfecting the world and oneself. This perfection of oneself, so as to make oneself fit to return to the One, takes many lifetimes or transmigrations. During this time it appears that the person is a separate individual, but this individuality ceases when one merges back into the Ein-Sof.

Although these two ideas of self-identity seem quite different, on analysis they can be seen to be very similar. For in the former case the creation comes from the thought and command of God. This concept of 'creatio ex nihilo – creation out of nothing – is at the core of Judaism's belief in a divine Creator.'[23] This is likened to the big bang theory which is similar to the Kabbalist view of everything emanating from the Ein-Sof, the divine nothingness. This implies that all material, including dust, comes from nothingness and thus the material person comes from the same place as the Kabbalist soul. Both of these ideas of the person seem to have been created for the same reason and with the same function, that of being an instrument of the Divine to enjoy and continue with His creation whilst caring for others: His instruments. The main difference is that in the Kabbalist view the individual person goes through many reincarnations, whilst the orthodox view is that each person only exists for one lifetime. Orthodox Judaism has not spelt out how the material universe, or Creation, will end. If one accepts the big crunch theory in which the universe will finally contract to a single point, it could be argued that all material will also finally return to the One; and in this case the only difference in the two concepts of self-identity would boil down to the length of one's individual existence.

---

[23] Rabbi Benjamin Blech, *Understanding Judaism*, Indianapolis, 1999, p.4.

When one is identified as God's instrument or servant, filled with his 'breath' or life-force, one naturally follows His commandments with no concern for the future, as one is not identified as a separate individual ego. Or, to put it another way, one surrenders one's ego to God by keeping Him and His commandments in mind, following His will rather than one's own self-will. This leads to seeing the creation 'as it is' and not through the filter of narrow egoistic concerns, opinions and judgements. This makes it much easier to share His excitement and joy in everything He has put on this earth and thus to enjoy life. This identification, as God's instrument or servant, also stills the mind, making it easier to be aware of God and His presence so that one can truly be the flow of His force, the ebb and flow of His tides and in this live creatively. Also, one sees others as God's instruments, or servants, thus leading one to have love for one's neighbour as for one's self.

Conversely, if one sees:
-man as made in the image of God,
-that God is immanent,
-that God left his creation unfinished and thought 'that it was good',
-that two of man's purposes in life were to help further God's creation and enjoy life,
-finally that man is a purely ephemeral being (from dust to dust) animated by 'the breath of God', then one could easily conclude that man is purely an instrument of God. In this all humans are of like worth and nature and in the final analysis have no lasting separate identity.

Chapter Two
Christianity

In Christianity consideration is mainly given to fundamentalist Christians who believe in the literal truth of the Bible and to Catholicism which is the most widely adhered to of the various denominations. Christadelphianism is used as an example of a fundamentalist viewpoint, although other fundamentalists may interpret the literal truth of the Bible differently.

God

The Christian descriptions of the Absolute, in the New Testament, naturally have much in common with those in the Old Testament. God is described as 'One' (Mark 12 v.29, Galatians 3 v.20), 'Omniscient' (1 John 3 v.20), 'The Witness' (1 John 5 v.7-9, Romans 1 v.9), 'All Powerful' (1 John 5 v.4), 'Never been seen' or ineffable (John 1 v.18) and 'Spirit' (John 4 v.24). Thus God is transcendent, omnipotent, omniscient, omnipresent, ineffable spirit. In contrast to the Old Testament there are no references to other 'gods'. Also God is 'in us' (1 John 4 v.12 and many others) 'among (within) you' (Luke 17 v.21), 'all-giving (2 Corinthians 9 v.8), 'salvation' (Acts 28 v.28) and 'all-seeing' (Hebrews 4 v.12-14). So He is immanent in the world and the help and salvation of the just. He is the 'true judge' (Romans 2 v.2), 'the ruler and giver' (Romans 11 v.22), 'good and merciful' (Ibid), 'wrathful' (Revelations 15 v.1) and 'hates pride' (1 Peter 5 v.5). These highlight that we are accountable to God for our thoughts and actions. Other attributes of God are that He is 'love' (1 John 4 v.8), our 'Father' (John 14 v.6 and many more), 'light' (1 John 1 v.5) and an 'all burning (consuming) fire' (Hebrews 12 v.29). So God is our Father, full of light and love, in whom all pride, ego and ignorance are consumed.

This leaves the central or basic difference between Judaism and Christianity: the incarnation of God as man and the doctrine of the Holy Trinity. This is a great mystery which is not completely clarified by the scriptures. In Luke 12 v.10 we find: 'And whosoever shall speak a word against the Son of man (Jesus), it shall be forgiven him; but unto him that blasphemeth against the Holy Ghost it shall not be forgiven.' This indicates some degree of separation between Christ, God made flesh and the Holy Ghost, God as Spirit, although John (20 v.22) records that Christ had the power to bestow the Holy Ghost: 'And when he said this he breathed on them and saith unto them, Receive ye the Holy Ghost'. Mark also records some degree of difference between Christ (the Son) and 'the Absolute' (the Father): 'But of that day and hour knoweth no man ... neither the Son, but the Father' (Mark 13 v.32). Yet this is contradicted by Matthew when he says: 'And Jesus came and spake unto them saying, All power is given unto me in heaven and in earth. Go therefore and teach all nations, baptising them in the name of the Father and of the Son and of the Holy Ghost.' (Matthew 28 v.18-20). This seems to indicate three different entities and yet it is clear that this is not the case ('and these three are one', 1 John 5 v.7-10). Summing up, it appears that the Father, Holy Ghost and Christ are different aspects of The One (Absolute) but that Christ was somewhat subject to the restrictions of being made flesh.

Creation

The Christian view of creation is naturally based on that given in Genesis. Orthodox (or fundamentalist) Christians believe in the literal truth of the six-day creation story. However, many Christians believe that the creation story in Genesis is a mythical way of explaining the beginning of all things, whilst also accepting the theory of evolution. The six days of creation are read to mean 'six periods of time during which the creation took place'.[24] Christians also believe that the universe was created 'out of nothing' (creatio ex nihilo): 'By faith we perceive that the universe was fashioned by the word of God so that the visible came forth from the invisible'. (Hebrews 11 v.3) This concept is equated with the 'big bang' theory by many non-fundamental Christians. There is also some evidence in the New Testament which suggests that Jesus was intimately connected with the creation:

> In him (Jesus) everything in heaven and earth was created ... the whole universe has been created through him and for him. And he exists before everything and all things are held together in him. (Colossians 1 v.16-17)

However, this should not be read to imply that Jesus, the man, created the world, but to show his oneness with God: 'He is the image of the invisible God; his is the primacy over all created things.' (Colossians 1 v.15) This passage also gives a clue as to one of the purposes of creation, in that the universe was created 'for him', implying that the creation took place in order that Jesus could be born to save mankind:

---

[24] Anne Geldart, Christianity, *Oxford*, 1999, p.41.

> Through him God chose to reconcile the whole universe to himself, making peace through the shedding of his blood upon the cross - to reconcile all things, whether on earth or in heaven, through him alone. (Colossians 1 v.20)

This ties in with the other purposes for creation, to manifest God's glory and for the happiness of man. Louis Berkhof, a Calvinist theologian, writes:

> Some find the final end or purpose of creation in the happiness of man ... The Bible teaches us clearly that God created the world for the manifestation of His glory. Naturally the revelation of the glory of God is not intended as an empty show to be admired by the creatures but also aims at promoting their welfare and attuning their hearts to the praise of the Creator.[25]

This is also in agreement with Catholic teaching, as Saint Irenaeus wrote, 'In the beginning God formed Adam not because He was in need of humans, but so that He might have someone to receive his benefits' (Against Heresies 4.14.1). Also in the acts and decrees of Vatican 1 (Collectio Lacencis, v.11.116) it states that: 'He made a creature that by its very nature would give glory to God even though God gains nothing by that glory'.[26] So by the 'saving of mankind' through the shedding of Christ's blood upon the cross God is glorified and mankind is benefited. However, only those who accept Christ as their saviour are benefited.

---

[25] Louis Berkhof, A *Summary of Christian Doctrine*, London, 1938, p.48.
[26] Rev William G. Most, *Creation and Angels*, www.ewtn.com/faith/teachings/goda32.htm

The Nature of Man

When it comes to how Christianity sees the nature of man there are divergent views, especially as to whether man has an immortal soul. Many fundamentalists hold to the Judaic view that man is just a material creature which is animated by the breath of God and which ceases to exist on the death of the body. They read the word 'soul', as translated in many versions of the Bible, to mean the bodily person which is subject to death and not an immortal individual spiritual essence which survives after the body is finished. As far as the 'spirit' is concerned this is equated with the life-force which God 'breathes' into man and which He withdraws upon the death of the body. However, man can gain conditional immortality 'through the work of Christ... The only way to gain immortality is through obedience to God's commands.'[27]

Most non-fundamentalists do believe in a noncorporeal immortal soul which continues after death. There are three basic views of the origin of the soul in each person: pre-existentialism, which states that souls existed in a previous state before being born in a body; Traducianism, which holds that the soul is derived from one's parents (as is the body); and creationism, which is the view that the soul is created by God and placed in the body.[28] The Catholics believe in the last view and hold that infusion, the uniting of the body and soul, occurs at conception. This accounts for their staunch opposition to an abortion at any stage

---

[27] Duncan Heaster, *Bible Basics,* Birmingham, 2000, p111.
[28] Louis Berkhof, A *Summary of Christian Doctrine, London*, 1938, p.62.

in pregnancy. They also believe that God had given to Adam and Eve three gifts which were to be passed on to humanity: (1) body and soul with mind and will, a co-ordinating gift through which man could keep his basic drives in check. This gift included (2) exemption from physical death, plus (3) the gift of grace 'which made the soul capable of the vision of God in the life to come.'[29] However, by the sin of eating the forbidden fruit, they fell from his favour, losing the last two gifts and thus only transmitting the first gift, basic humanity, to their progeny. Catholics believe that through Christ these two lost gifts may be recovered: 'He gives man the possibility of living in sanctifying grace. In the wake of His victory over sin He also takes away the dominion of death.'[30] The soul itself is an immaterial spiritual entity which is undetectable by the senses, can exist separate from the body, and will never die.

The Purpose of Life

Catholics also believe that the purpose of life is intimately connected with their interpretation of the purpose of creation. Man's purposes are to 'receive His benefits' and to 'all be saved and come to the knowledge of the truth' (1 Timothy 2 v.4). The third purpose is to 'give Glory to God even though God gains nothing by that glory'.[31] We become capable of receiving God's gifts by being saved through Christ

---

[29] Rev William G. Most, *The Creation Nature and Fall of Man,* www.ewtn.com/faith/teachings/goda42.htm
[30] Rev William G. Most, *Christ conquers the Evil of Death,* www.ewtn.com/faith/teachings/deatha1.htm
[31] Rev William G. Most, *Creation and Angels,* www.ewtn.com/faith/teachings/goda32.htm

and giving glory to God. This receptivity is enhanced by following what Catholics call 'The Great Commandment':

> You shall love the Lord god with your whole heart, with your whole soul and with your whole mind. This is the greatest and the first commandment. The second is like it: 'You shall love your neighbour as yourself. (Matthew 22 v.37-38)

This may be called another purpose, that of loving God and one's fellow man, although it may also be considered to be a way of achieving the fulfilment of man's primary purposes.

It is not only Catholics who call this the 'greatest commandment'; as Anne Geldart says: 'Love of God cannot be separated from love of Humanity. Some Christians go even further and say that people must try to love all of creation, not just human life.'[32]

Christadelphians believe that man's purposes revolve around 'living a life which is fitting for someone who has the hope of being given God's nature (2 Peter 1 v.4) and of actually sharing His name (Revelations 3 v.12) through being made perfect in every way.'[33] To achieve this they place particular emphasis on baptism, gaining perfection or holiness by overcoming fleshly tendencies, following Christ's example, Bible study, prayer and participating in the life of the Church. These may be called secondary purposes, the aim of which is 'to enter God's Kingdom'.[34]

---

[32] Anne Geldart, Christianity, *Oxford*, 1999, p.63.
[33] Duncan Heaster, *Bible Basics,* Birmingham, 2000, p.319.
[34] Ibid, p.319-342.

Once again it is not only fundamentalists who stress these objectives, the essence of Christianity being to follow Christ's examples and teachings - as Christ said: 'You must be perfect just as your Father in heaven is perfect.' (Matthew 5 v.48) Most denominations also place emphasis on baptism, prayer and participating in the life of the Church. These purposes and methods can all be summed as ways of doing 'God's Will' so that we may become receptive of 'God's gifts', glorify God and enter His kingdom. In this way God's will may 'be done on earth as it is in heaven'. (Matthew 6 v.10) For Thomas Merton, that famous contemporary Trappist monk, this entails totally giving oneself to God:

> If I am to know the will of God I must have the right attitude towards life...giving myself to God... is the real meaning of His will. He does not need our sacrifices, He asks for our selves.[35]

The Afterlife

With regard to what happens at death there are many divergent opinions within Christianity. Christadelphians believe that death is the complete and final end, except for those 'that can find a way to gain eternal life and immortality through the work of Christ.'[36] This occurs at The Day of Judgement when not only the living, but also the 'responsible dead', are resurrected and judged. These include only those who have known or understood the word of Christ and so were able to accept or reject him. The righteous will be saved whereas the

---

[35] Thomas Merton, *No Man is an Island, in* Lucinda Vardey's, 'God in All Worlds' Alexandria (AUS), 1995, p.396.
[36] Duncan Heaster, *Bible Basics,* Birmingham, 2000, p.112.

wicked will die a death of total unconsciousness which will be everlasting. In this regard there is no belief in purgatory or in hell as a place of eternal suffering.[37] They also believe that the saved will live in 'God's Kingdom' on earth, which will never be destroyed but will be renewed by God fulfilling his promise: 'Behold I create a new heavens and a new earth'. (Isaiah 65 v.17)[38]

Catholics, however, due to their belief in an immortal soul, maintain that the body dies but that the soul survives separated from the body. When one dies, one will be judged immediately with the possible outcome that the soul will go to heaven, purgatory or hell. However, there will be a second coming of Christ, the Parousia, when a final judgement will take place on those who are still alive.[39] The present Pope, Benedict XVI, states that heaven is not some metaphysical region where the saved will reside but 'is to be defined as the contact of the being "man" with the being "God" ... the reality of heaven only comes into existence through the confluence of God and man.'[40] The previous Pope, John Paul II, agrees with this in saying that heaven is 'neither an abstraction nor a physical place in the clouds, but a living personal relationship with the Holy Trinity.'[41] In like fashion he states that 'rather than a place hell indicates the state of those who separate themselves from God, the source of all life and joy'.[42] This is also in

---

[37] Ibid, p.132.
[38] Ibid p.103-105.
[39] Rev William G. Most, *Particular Judgement,* www.ewtn.com/faith/teachings/judgea1.htm
[40] Joseph Cardinal Ratzinger, *Introduction to Christianity,* San Francisco, 2004, p.313-314.
[41] Pope John Paul II, *Heaven Hell and Purgatory,* www.ewtn.com/library/PAPALDOC/JP2HEAVEN.htm#Heaven
[42] *Ibid*

accord with the views of most modern theologians who speak in terms of hell as 'separation from God' although some do, in agreement with the Christadelphians, speak of hell as ceasing to exist, which is the fate of those who have been unable to obtain 'conditional immortality.'[43]

Analysis

Prior to analysing the correlation between self-identity and world-view in the two denominations being considered, we sum up the two concepts of self-identity that have been enunciated. The Christadelphian view is of man as a physical being who is animated by 'the breath of God' and who dies when this is withdrawn. However, that there is the possibility of resurrection indicates that humans have a personal-essence which survives death, albeit unconsciously, and can be reborn. Quite how or where this 'essence' survives is not clear, certainly not in the original body which decomposes after death; maybe in the 'mind of God' from which everything is created. This essence is rather like the software (in a computer) which cannot function without its compatible hardware. So this essence, having been 'stored' on the death of the original body, can only function in a compatible body which must be reborn on the Day of Judgement. The Catholic view, by comparison, is pure Descartian dualism in which the essence is an immortal soul placed in a physical body which survives and lives independently after the death of that body.

---

[43] John Young, *Christianity (Teach Yourself World Faiths)*, Abingdon, 1996, p.121.

Catholics basically link the purpose of creation with the purpose of human life, in that the creation is for the manifestation of God's glory and for the benefit of man who can in return give glory to and praise God. Thus humans (souls) are created to achieve this aim and if they succeed they will receive their just reward by going to heaven, or purgatory if further purification is required. Failing this, the soul will survive eternally but 'forever completely separate from God'. The soul is also created to be the beneficiary of God's gifts and as all souls are created for the same purposes, man is enjoined to love his fellow man as well as God, his benefactor. Thomas Merton states that to achieve these aims one must totally give oneself to God and this is born out by Matthew 16 v.24-26:

> If anyone wishes to be a follower of mine, he must leave his self behind... if a man let himself be lost for my sake, he will find his true self. What will a man gain by winning the whole world at the cost of his true self? Or what can he give that will buy that self back?

So to follow Christ, according to this Catholic version, one must give up one's ego, or small self, and lose oneself totally. This losing oneself is focussed on giving up one's pride and ego so that one becomes truly capable of receiving God's benefits and giving glory to Him. For it is pride ('consciousness of one's own dignity, the quality of having an excessively high opinion of oneself'[44]) and ego which separate us from God and prevent us from conforming to His will. To truly know the will of God we need to come near enough to Him for these to be consumed in the 'all burning fire' that God is (Hebrews 12 v.29).

---

[44] *Compact Oxford English Dictionary*, Oxford, 2003, p. 897.

Christadelphians believe that the main purpose of humanity is to become 'perfect' through obedience to God's will and so the overcoming of pride and ego is also important for them. As Jesus said: 'Take my yoke and become like me, for I am gentle and without pride and you will have rest' (Matthew 11 v.29). To become 'perfect as your Father in heaven is perfect' (Matthew 5 v.48) requires that humans put aside their opinions, preferences and knowledge and become completely aligned to the will of God. This is even more critical for Christadelphians, as the result of failure is complete extinction, whereas for the Catholic there is a second chance of achieving this perfection in purgatory.

In the final analysis both Catholics and Christadelphians believe that there is some kind of 'personal essence' in human beings, although they are of very different types. This essence can be perfected and 'has the hope of being given God's nature' (2Peter1 v.4). Through this process one becomes worthy of receiving His gifts and giving worship and thanksgiving to Him for these gifts and the whole of creation. Thus by completing the purpose for which they are created humans can be saved and be rewarded by entering God's Kingdom whether that is in Heaven or on Earth. Therefore with both these views of self-identity, if one adopts and follows the world-view specified by the denomination in question, one is promised life eternal.

Chapter Three

Islam

This chapter will consider orthodox Muslim views based on the Qur'an and those of the Sufis, the mystical arm of Islam. The Sufis comprise many different sects, each with its own practices, all of which have the same aim: that of achieving union with God whilst alive, and this is to be realized by attaining 'the death of the conventional self' (*fana*).[45]

God

The first thing to be said about how Islam views God, Allah, is that the Qur'an makes it quite clear that He is 'not the messiah, son of Mary' (Q 5 v.17 and 72). Islam has great regard for Jesus as a prophet, but Muslims do not believe that he was the son of God: 'The Messiah, Jesus son of Mary, was only a messenger of Allah ... Far is it removed from his Transcendental Majesty that He should have a son. Allah is only One God.' (Q 1v.171).

As Islam accepts much of the Old Testament and the Gospels, whilst asserting that the Qur'an is the latest and final revelation which corrects errors in the former, it is not surprising that Allah, the Absolute, is described in very similar ways as God is in the Bible. Allah is 'all

---

[45] Mohammad Shafii, *Freedom From The Self,* New York, 1985 p.239.

powerful' (Q 2 v.109 and many others), 'all hearing and all knowing '(Q 2 v.181 and many), 'everlasting' (Q 20 v.73), 'the truth (the only reality)' (Q 31 v.30), the 'only One God, (Q 2 v.163 and many) and 'independent of all the worlds (of all his creatures)' (Q 3 v.97). So the Absolute is omnipotent, omniscient, eternal, One and transcendent. He is 'the creator of everything' (Q 13 v.16), 'the lighter of the heavens and the earth' (Q 21 v.35), 'the king (sovereign) of the heavens and the earth' (Q 5 v.17-18) and 'all things belong to him' (Q 1 v.131 and many). Thus he is the creator, ruler and owner of all of manifestation. Also He is 'between the man and his own heart' (Q 8 v.24), 'among/with you' (Q 67 v.35 and many), 'the seer of what they do' (Q 2 v.96 and many) and 'able to send a sign' (Q 6 v.37). Therefore Allah is immanent, aware of all of man's thoughts and deeds and able to respond to them. Allah helps the just and believers by being 'bountiful' (Q 2 v.251 and many), their 'guardian/protector' (Q 2 v.257 and many), their 'embracer (carer) and knower' (Q 2 v.268 and many), 'helper' (Q 1v.45), 'guide' (Q 22 v.16 and many), 'patient' (Q 8 v.46 and many) and 'sufficient for you' (Q 8 v.62 and many).

For the believer, Allah provides everything that is needed and, in material lack, He alone is sufficient. He is also the judge of mankind being 'firm and punishing' (Q 2 v.211 and many), 'swift in reckoning' (Q 3 v.19 and many), 'mighty and vengeful' (Q 3 v.4 and many) counterbalanced by being 'merciful and bounteous' (Q 2 v.105 and many), 'forgiving and merciful' (Q 2 v.173 and many) and 'never unjust to his worshippers.' (Q 3 v.182).

Other properties assigned to Allah are those of being 'rich (free of all wants)' (Q 1v.131 and many), 'True in speech' (Q 1v.122), 'my worshipful Lord' (Q 3 v.51), 'the sender of the winds' (Q30 v.9), 'high, great' (Q 1v.34) and the 'enemy of the unbelievers' (Q 2 v.98). While Allah is transcendent, omnipotent, omniscient and eternal, He is also immanent and intervenes to help or punish us as we deserve. Allah, as so described, is very similar to the God of Judaism and also that of 'The Father' of the Christian trinity.

The Sufis have developed a more mystical concept of Allah as being the Absolute which has manifested Himself in, and as, the universe - 'a God who is the creative principle and ultimate ground of all that exists'.[46] Hallaj, the great Sufi mystic who was crucified for daring to identify himself with God or the Truth, conceived of Allah as love who before creation loved Himself in absolute oneness. He desired to behold that love through and as an external object so He created out of nothingness a divine image of Himself, Adam, who could love and glorify Him.[47] Jili likened the universe to ice and God to the water in which the ice exists; so that although it may appear that forms and the Absolute are different, 'we mystics know they are the same'.[48] This gives the key to the Sufi practice of *fana* or loss of self, through which one can realize oneness with the Absolute, or union with God, by overcoming the misidentification of one's essence as being mind, ego, or body.

---

[46] R.A. Nicholson, *Studies in Islamic Mysticism*, Cambridge, 1921 p.79.
[47] Ibid, p. 80.
[48] Ibid p. 99.

Creation

Muslims basically believe the Biblical account of creation, that Allah created the heavens and earth and all that is between them, in six days. (Q 7 v.54) However, the Arabic word *youmm* (day) can mean a period of time, In Surah 70 v.4 it means 50,000 years, so Muslims tend to believe that creation took place in six distinct phases, each one taking an indeterminate length of time. This creation could well have started with the big bang, as it says in the Qur'an: 'the heavens and earth were joined together as one unit, before We clove them asunder' (Q 21 v.30).[49] Surah 7 v.54 also shows that everything in the universe is under the command of, or follows the orders of, Allah - its creator. Moreover, 'the Koranic conception of God is as a creator who is never absent from this creation and who nurtures and tends to every atom in existence continually,'[50] so that were Allah to stop nurturing any created thing, it would cease to exist. Muslims believe in continuous creation in which Allah is continually creating and re-creating the universe, annihilating and re-creating everything continuously in such miniscule periods of time that the manifestation seems to be semi-permanent.[51] Martin Lings asserts that one of the most central Qur'anic teachings is: 'Do not look on the things of this world as independent realities for they are all in fact entirely dependent for their existence on the Hidden Treasure whose Glory they were created to reveal'. He backs this up by quoting Surah 17 v.44. This Hidden Treasure, according to the Hadith, 'desired to be known therefore I created the

---

[49] http:/islam.about.com/od/creation/a/creation.htm
[50] Colin Turner, *Islam The Basics,* London, 2006, p.76.
[51] Ibid p. 77.

creatures in order that I might be known.'[52]

The Nature of Man

According to the Sufi Jili, man is created in the image of God and the universe is created in the image of man; not only that, but man represents the world-spirit so that when mankind exits from the universe it will perish in the same way that an animal dies when the spirit leaves.[53] Man is made in the image of God, so he is unique in creation and has the potential to be the vessel through which the Hidden Treasure might be known, in fact can know itself. This can only occur when man stops identifying himself as a separate individual and realizes his oneness with the Absolute.[54] In other words, this represents the mystical interpretation of the Godhead and its relationship to humanity. In Sufism, man is considered to be a complete microcosm, a miniature universe, containing all the elements and potential qualities of creation. For him the universe was created, and he was created, to serve God.

Muslims believe that man, as made by God, is pure, free from any original sin and is naturally inclined to be righteous and serve God. [55] However, when caught in the snare of superstition, customs, selfish desires and false teachings, he can easily revert to the animal level of greed, lust and selfishness.[56] As to whether man has an immortal soul

---

[52] Martin Lings, *What Is Sufism?*, London, 1975, p.57.
[53] R.A. Nicholson, *Studies in Islamic Mysticism*, Cambridge, 1921, p.121.
[54] Ibid p. 127.
[55] http:/muslim-canada.org/sufi/sufism.htm

separate from the body, the Muslim position is not clear. There are many references in the Qur'an to 'killing souls', and it is stated quite clearly that 'every soul shall taste death' (Q 21 v.35 and 29 v.57). Muslims believe that when one dies, the body is destroyed, but the essence of a person goes into a kind of limbo state of semi-consciousness (*barzakh*) awaiting the day of resurrection. This is not the same as the Descartian view of the soul as a separate entity, for this essence still requires a body which will be provided on the day of resurrection.[57] However, those who are judged the foremost of the foremost transcend this need for a body and achieve 'union with God Himself in a realm that is beyond comprehension and description.'[58]

This does indicate some kind of spiritual essence which can exist permanently separate from a body, but only when it achieves such purity that it can be reabsorbed back into the Godhead. To indicate this essence Sufis use the word *nafs* which means breath, life-force, soul, spirit, self, individual substance and pure essence. There are different levels of *nafs* through which one must pass on the journey to union with the divine such as mineral, vegetable, animal and various levels of human development.[59] This is beautifully illustrated by Rumi, the great Sufi poet, who wrote:

> I died as a mineral and became a plant,
> I died as a plant and became an animal,
> I died as an animal and became a man,
> What is there to fear? When have I ever become less by dying?
> And as a man I shall die once more to soar
> With the blessed Angels, but even from angelhood

---

[56] http:/webpages.marshall.edu/~laher1/intro.html
[57] Maulana Muhammad Ali, *The Religion of Islam,* Lahore, 1950, p.271-282.
[58] Colin Turner, *Islam The Basics,* London, 2006, p.93.
[59] Mohammad Shafii, *Freedom From The Self,* New York, 1985 p.20-21.

I must pass on; Everything perishes save His Face
And when I have given up my angel soul
I shall become that which no mind has ever grasped.
So let me not exist!
For non-existence proclaims in organ tones:

'From Him we come and to Him we shall return.'[60]

This journey takes place by the purification of the self so that one returns to that original purity of man created in the image of God. The contemporary Turkish Sufi Said Nursi, who is well known for his 5,000 page Epistle of Light collection of commentaries on the Qur'an, has an interesting opinion on the nature of this self as 'an abstract entity whose sole function is to act as a kind of yardstick against which God's names or attributes can be measured.'[61] Through one's own limited attributes one can extrapolate from them God's attributes as being similar but on a much vaster cosmic scale. The 'I' is a mirror-like device through which one can affirm the existence of and glimpse, the Absolute. It is when one takes the 'I' to be a real separate entity, which claims individual ownership of its attributes, that one falls and is cut off from God.[62]

The Purpose of Life

---

[60] Colin Turner, *Islam The Basics,* London, 2006, p.90-91.
[61] Ibid p. 154.
[62] Ibid, p.155-159.

Ziauddin Sardar believes that the purpose of life is to 'do good and spread goodness on earth' by obeying God and following his commandments'[63]. In fact the word Islam means submission and points to this purpose of submitting to the will of God. Other thinkers quote the Qur'an, saying that man is created to be Allah's trustee on earth (Q 2 v.30) and to worship the creator (Q 51 v.56-58). Muslims also believe that this life is a test or trial, an 'examination for the individual', the purpose of which is to determine one's final resting place after death.[64] The way to achieve all of the above purposes and attain a favourable outcome when one is judged, is to hold to the five pillars of Islam by accepting and following the 'five essential and obligatory practices': the shahada or the profession of faith, praying five times a day facing Mecca at the prescribed times, giving alms to the needy, fasting from dawn to sunset during the month of Ramadan and performing the Hajj, the pilgrimage to Mecca, at least once.[65]

For the Sufi however, whilst the previous purposes are valid, the ultimate purpose is to achieve union with God by overcoming the separation caused by identification as a unique individual entity, 'I'. The aim is to return to our origin, God: 'From Him we come and to Him we shall return'. Man was created and animated by God (and his breath) so 'Sufis feel that God's life-giving breath bestows on human beings the potential for existential communion, the oneness of all with All.'[66] Shaykh Fadhalla Haeri says that the constant recognition of this unity

---

[63] Ziauddin Sardar, *What Muslims Believe,* London, 2006, p.42.
[64] www.islamtomorrow.com/purpose.htm
[65] John Esposito, *Islam The Straight Path,* Oxford, 1998, p.88-92.
[66] Mohammad Shafii, *Freedom From The Self,* New York, 1985 p.48.

in creation is the ultimate purpose of life. This is to be achieved by willingly and knowingly surrendering and submitting to Allah and results in the personalty melting into the 'total flow of events'. [67] Sufis follow many different practices to achieve their aim including holding to the five pillars, constant remembrance of God, the development of ecstatic love for God, losing themselves in ritual dancing and chanting, meditation, purification of the mind and body, repetition of the many names of God and going on extended spiritual retreats.[68]

The Afterlife

Muslims believe there are six basic components to the afterlife: the semi-conscious limbo state (*barzakh*) where one awaits the Day of Judgement, resurrection into recreated bodies, judgement, heaven, hell and union with (absorption into) God. The Day of Judgement is mentioned many times in the Qur'an, some examples being: '... till the Day of Resurrection. Then to Me you shall all return and I shall judge between you'. (Q 3 v.55) 'And when the Horn is blown, on that Day (of Judgement)... those whose scales (of acquired merit) are heavy shall prosper, but those whose scales are light shall forfeit their souls and live in Gehenna (Hell) for ever.' (Q 23 v.101-108)

Muslims believe in bodily resurrection, a time when people will arise from their graves in recreated physical bodies to be judged according to their deeds and beliefs in the 'first life'.[69] There are many references

---

[67] Shaykh Fadhalla Haeri, *The Thoughtful Guide To Sufism,* Alresford (UK), 2004, p.91.
[68] Ibid, p.55-79.

in the Qur'an to this resurrection of the body, some examples being: 'He revives the earth after its death.... As for the dead, Allah will revive them. To Him they shall return.' (Q 6 v.35-36) and 'He brings out the living from the dead... He revives the earth after its death. Likewise you shall be brought forth.' (Q 30 v.19) The resurrected will be judged by Allah alone 'according to the record found in the Book of deeds.' (Q 45 v.29-30) This judgement will either consign one to hell, heaven, or to be with Allah.

Hell is a place of physical torment and fire: 'the fire tastes their face and therein are shrivelled lips' (Q 23 v.104) and 'except for he who shall roast in Hell' (Q 37 v.163), whilst heaven is described as a 'Garden of Delight' where the inhabitants...

> sitting face to face upon couches,
> a goblet from a spring shall be passed round to them,
> a delight to the drinkers,
> and with them will be maidens
> who restrain their wide glances as if they were hidden pearls.
> (Q 37 v.43-49)

However, to be assigned to be 'with Allah is the best return,' (Q 3 v.14) for 'with Allah is the reward of the world and of the Everlasting Life.' (Q 4 v.134) That this union with Allah is reserved for the chosen few is shown here: 'the abode of the Everlasting Life is with Allah for you especially, to the exclusion of all other people.' (Q 2 v.94)

The Sufis basically accept these mainstream Muslim beliefs but attempt to enter union with the beloved whilst still alive. By self-abnegation they live in and with Allah and thus gain eternal life, for

---

[69] www.nderf.org/islamic_views_nde.htm (Afterlife)

Allah, the source of all life and existence, never dies. Massood Ali Khan puts it this way:

> A Sufi understands from the idea of self-negation an attainment of perpetual existence. He 'dies' in the body so that he may live for ever in the spirit. He dies in this world so that he may live forever in the next. He dies from self so that he may live in God.[70]

This death is not of the body but of the self or ego, and the attainment of life in the next world is achieved whilst still alive. This merger of one's essence with God is achieved whilst still living and continues after the death of the physical body. About this, the 13th century Sufi mystic Nasafi wrote:

> The prophets and the Sufi... experience death of the conventional self (*fana*) before dying a natural death. They die voluntarily before dying naturally. They see and experience before dying what other people experience after natural death.[71]

Analysis

Summing up, the orthodox Muslim view of self-identity is very similar to the fundamental Christian view that man has an essence which is preserved on the death of the body and will be restored to a resurrected body on the day of judgement. This will then live on forever either in heaven or hell unless one is judged among the foremost of the foremost in which case one transcends the body and is united with

---

[70] Masood Ali Khan, *Sufism in Islam,* New Delhi, 2003, p.306.
[71] Mohammad Shafii, *Freedom From The Self,* New York, 1985 p.239.

Allah. Sufis hold similar views but believe that this union can occur whilst one is still alive and continue after death.

Man was created with the main purpose of knowing the Hidden Treasure (Allah) who created the world to reveal His glory. Allah's purpose in creating man was as an instrument to know himself by loving and glorifying Allah and His creation. Before creation Allah was One, so He created many images of Himself through which He could know Himself. This ties in with Said Nursi's idea of man as a mirror-like device through which Allah can be glimpsed by extrapolating His attributes from one's own but on a much vaster scale. For this to occur one needs to submit totally to the will of Allah so that one does not 'cloud the mirror' with one's own ego or opinions. In this state one can act as a pure instrument of Allah, worshipping Him and being His trustee on earth.

For the orthodox Muslim, man exists as a separate individual being that, although made in the image of God, will remain forever separate from Allah whilst alive and except in a few exceptional cases, namely 'the foremost of the foremost', will remain eternally separate after death in heaven or hell. However, for the Sufi the purpose of life is to attain spiritual union with Allah whilst alive, resulting in complete union on death when one ceases to exist as a separate being:

> So let me not exist!
> For non-existence proclaims in organ tones:
> 'From Him we come and to Him we shall return'.

Therefore the major difference in the view of self-identity between orthodox Muslims and the Sufis is that, whilst both hold that we are made in the image of God, the former believe, except in a few exceptional cases, that we exist forever as separate beings, whereas the latter hold that we are, in reality, never separate from Allah. This is because Allah is the creative principal and ultimate ground of all that exists and, although it may appear that creation and the Absolute are different, the Sufis, through their mystical practices and insights, know they are the same.

As can be seen, the world-view and concept of self-identity are inextricably linked for both the Muslim and the Sufi, for Allah created the world so that He could know Himself and man was created for this purpose alone. The way of life for the Muslim and the Sufi is designed with this in mind so that one can always remember Allah through glorifying Him and His creation. That this creation is not static but continuous means that the material world is not an independent reality, but continually reveals the divine presence and the glory of the Hidden Treasure. For the Muslim the purpose is to appreciate the creation and its creator by aligning with the will of Allah and by continual submission so that one loses one's identification as a separate ego in order that one can become a perfect vessel or mirror through which Allah can love and know Himself.

Chapter Four
Hinduism

Hinduism may be viewed not as one religion but a vast variety of streams or paths leading to liberation or God realization which evolved on the Indian sub-continent from the ancient Vedic religion of Brahmanism and the pre-existing religions of the subcontinent. These were based on the Vedas, a collection of scriptures written between about 1500 and 500 BCE.[72] This book considers two of these streams the first of which, Advaita Vedanta, is based on the Upanishads, which represent 'the last works of the Vedas, the final stage of Vedic evolution ... where the emphasis is away from ritual and theology and towards the personal and mystical experiencing of the One'.[73] Advaita means nonduality and Vedanta means 'the end of the Vedas', so Advaita Vedanta is a form of nondualism based on the books at 'the end of the Vedas', which are the Upanishads.

The second stream to be considered is a dualistic approach based on the worship of Vishnu and his many descents or *avatars*. There are many different forms of this worship, known as Vaishnavism, depending on which incarnation (*avatar*) of Vishnu is being worshipped and on the lineage of the guru or preceptor of each particular sect. The form to be considered here is that of Gaudiya Vaishnavism, founded in 1886, claiming descent from Jiva Goswami, one of the six Goswamis who were the direct disciples of Chaitanya (1486-1534) responsible for

---

[72] J. Hinnells, *Living Religions*, 1997, London, p.264
[73] Ibid, p.266

formulating and recording his philosophy. Their followers worship Krishna first and foremost, and also Chaitanya who is regarded as a descent of Vishnu and through whom Krishna is said to have manifested himself. They use many different scriptural texts, the oldest and most revered of which is the Bhagavad Gita. The most well known disciple of this movement is A.C.Bhaktivedanta Swami Prabhupada, hereafter called Bhaktivedanta, who wrote many books and commentaries on the Vaishnavic scriptures.

God

In the Upanishads the Absolute, Brahman, is the source and creator of all manifestation (i.e. all universes) but also *is* everything within that manifestation:
1. 'Before the world was created the Self (Brahman) alone existed; nothing whatever stirred. Then the Self thought: "Let me create the world".
2. He brought forth all the worlds out of himself
Aitareya Upanishad (from the *Rig-Veda*) Part 1, Ch.1 v.1-2.

Not only is Brahman the universe, its origin and cause, but eventually all will return to him:
'This universe comes forth from Brahman and will return to Brahman, verily all is Brahman' (*Chandogya* III 14.1). This can be compared to the singularity, which exploded in the big bang to create the universe, which will eventually contract back to a singularity in the big crunch. Thus the totality of cosmic energy rests at a single point, manifests into

the universe which is composed of cosmic energy itself, and then contracts back into a single point.

As Brahman is everything, it follows that we all are Brahman and that He is the agent by which the mind thinks, eye sees, tongue speaks, ear hears and body breathes (*Kena* I v.5-9). He is also described as the 'ear of the ear, eye of the eye, mind of the mind, word of the words and life of the life' (*Kena* I v.2). Thus He is the 'pure awareness' (*Brihadaranyaka* 4 v.7) in which all thought, life and sensation appears; and He is the 'seer' (*Isha* v.8) and 'all knowing' (*Katha* 2 v.18).

He is also described as 'one' (*Isha* v.4), 'radiant, everywhere, transcendent, indivisible, pure' (v.8). As the cause, existence and dissolution of everything that exists, He is 'immortal, eternal, immutable' (*Katha* 2 v.18), 'without beginning or end, beyond time and space' (3 v.15), 'infinite, imperishable and unborn' (*Mundaka* II 1.1 & 1.2). Although He is 'within all' *(Isha* v.5) and 'the light of man' (*Brihadaranyaka* IV v.6) He is also 'unseeable, ineffable and unknowable' (*Kena* v.3). This is because He is 'pure consciousness' (*Aitareya* ch.3 v.1) and the 'attributeless reality' (*Svetasvetara* ch. 3 v.1). Thus all attributes appear in, exist in and disappear back into Brahman, but having no attributes He is unperceivable by the mind and the senses. Thus this 'pure awareness', Brahman, is the substratum and essence of all of existence.[74]

---

[74] E. Easwaran, *The Upanishads*, 1988, Penguin, New Delhi

Bhaktivedanta states that the Absolute has three different aspects: Brahman, *Paramatman* and Bhagavan, which he backs up by quoting the *Srimad Bhagavatam*: 'Learned transcendentalists who know the Absolute Truth call this nondual substance Brahman, *Paramatman* or Bhagavan' (1.2.11). Of these he says that Bhagavan, Krishna the Personality of Godhead, is the last word in Absolute Truth whilst the impersonal Brahman represents the glow or effulgence of this Godhead and the *Paramatman* is the partial representation of this which may be realized in the human heart as the *atman*.[75] Moreover, the Bhagavad Gita states quite clearly that Krishna is the Ultimate Truth: 'There is no truth superior to Me (Krishna). Everything rests on me as pearls are strung on a thread' (7 v.7).

Krishna has the ability to take on any form and this allows him to be identified with virtually any deity or *avatar* in Hinduism. Thus Krishna may be worshipped in many personal forms and also as the impersonal Brahman, so this form of Vaishnavism 'is able to reconcile ideas of the dualistic Sankhya and Yoga systems with the nondualistic Vedanta'.[76]

The Bhagavad Gita describes Krishna variously as: omnipresent (9 v.4), the sustainer and protector of all beings (9 v.5), the source and abode of all beings (9 v.6), omniscient and omnipotent (9 v.18), the totality of all that exists (10 v.20-42), infinite, without beginning or end (11 v.19), unmanifest and imperishable (8 v.20) and undecaying, the preserver and primeval being (11 v.18).[77] Thus Krishna has all the

---

[75] A.C. Bhaktivedanta, *Dharma*, 1998, Los Angeles, p43-45.
[76] J. Stillson Judah, *Hare Krishna and the Counterculture,* 1974, New York, p.51.

qualities assigned to the impersonal Brahman plus those of a personal being that can and should be approached by devotion. This devotion, or *bhakti*, is the key practice of Vaishnavism.

Creation

Advaita Vedantists teach that Brahman *is* the creation, everything in manifestation, as well as being its origin, cause and final dissolution:

> The Lord of Love (Brahman) willed: "Let there be many!"
> He who has no form assumed many forms;
> He who is infinite appeared finite;
> He who is everywhere assumed a place;
> He who is all wisdom caused ignorance;
> He who is real caused unreality.
> It is He who gives reality to all.
> Before the universe was created,
> Brahman existed as unmanifest.
> (Taittiriya Upanishad Part II 6.1-7.1)

This creation occurs in cycles, emanating from the One, expanding until it reaches a certain point, when it contracts back to a point. Then once again creation occurs, expands, and finally contracts back to the One, and so on ad infinitum. This occurs 'over an incalculable period of time',[78] and can be likened to a never ending series of big bangs, expansions, contractions and big crunches. The reason for this creation is that Brahman wills it: 'because He likes to; because He is free',[79] and its purpose is for His enjoyment and play. Also, the unmanifest Brahman wished to behold Himself and by manifesting into 'the many' He could achieve this.

---

[77] Swami Vireswarananda, *Srimad Bhagavad-Gita,* 1948, Madras, p250-311.
[78] Swami Vivekananda, *The Complete Works Vol 2,* 1989, Mayavati, p.239.
[79] Swami Vivekananda, *The Complete Works Vol 6,* 1989, Mayavati, p.55.

Gaudiya Vaishnavas also believe in cyclical creation, with each cycle being a 'breath of Vishnu' lasting four billion three hundred million years[80], and that Krishna created the material world by creating three different energies which assume the form of three different Vishnus. These are the Karanodakasayi Vishnu, *mahat-tattwa,* the total material energy; Garbodakasayi Vishnu, the energy which creates the many diverse forms; and Kshirodakasayi Vishnu, the *Paramatman,* which is the all-pervading supersoul 'who is present even within the atoms'.[81] These three Vishnus are incarnations of Krishna who direct the activities of the material world. The first is the 'cause of all causes and lies in the cosmic causal ocean beyond the highest spiritual world',[82] who becomes the cause of the universe by glancing towards *Maya,* Krishna's inferior energy. The second manifests as Brahma, Vishnu and Siva, which are known as the guna descents of Garbodakasayi Vishnu. Of these, Brahma creates, Vishnu preserves and Siva destroys the material universe. The third (Kshirodakasayi Vishnu) is the supersoul of all beings.[83]

Krishna's inferior energy is that which creates the material world and, according to Chaitanya's philosophy of bhedabheda, this energy is different from Krishna who is unaffected by it.[84] However, 'besides this inferior energy...there is a superior energy of Mine which consists of all living entities' (B.G. 7 v.5) who have the same quality of existence as

---

[80] J. Stillson Judah, *Hare Krishna and the Counterculture,* 1974, New York, p.57.
[81] A.C. Bhaktivedanta, *The Bhagavad Gita As It Is,* 1989, Los Angeles, p.124
[82] J. Stillson Judah, *Hare Krishna and the Counterculture,* 1974, New York, p.55.
[83] J. Stillson Judah, *Hare Krishna and the Counterculture,* 1974, New York, p.55-56.
[84] J. Stillson Judah, *Hare Krishna and the Counterculture,* 1974, New York, p.55.

the Supreme; this may be realized by becoming free from the influence of the inferior energy, thus attaining *mukti*, liberation.[85]

Bhaktivedanta states that 'Krishna created the material world for the conditioned souls to learn how to perform *yagnas* (sacrifices) for the satisfaction of Vishnu'.[86] The Bhagavad Gita gives the reason for this: 'Work done as a sacrifice for Vishnu has to be performed, otherwise work binds one to this material world. Therefore perform prescribed duties for His satisfaction and in that way you will remain unattached and free from bondage' (3 v.9). This sacrifice is done for Krishna's enjoyment, 'for I am the only enjoyer and the only object of sacrifice' (9 v.24), and so that the performer of the sacrifice may be liberated and free from bondage.

The Nature of Man

Advaita Vedanta regards man as a physical organism through which Brahman senses and experiences the world. The *Kena Upanishad* states that it is the Self (Brahman) which is the agent and witness through which the mind thinks and the senses experience sensations. However, this Self is undetectable by the mind and senses, being the substratum in which they appear, exist and disappear (1 v.1-9). Moreover, due to its undetectable nature, it is very easy for man to overlook his true nature and identify with the mind and body. The *Katha Upanishad* likens man to a chariot, of which the *atman* (the Self,

---

[85] A.C. Bhaktivedanta, *The Bhagavad Gita As It Is*, 1989, Los Angeles, p.125
[86] J. Stillson Judah, *Hare Krishna and the Counterculture*, 1974, New York, p.69.

Brahman within each individual) is the master, the body is the chariot, the mind is the charioteer, the sense organs are the horses and the roads they travel on are the objects of sensation. The *atman* is the enjoyer and experiencer of the ride which is made possible by the charioteer, chariot and horses (3 v.3-4). So Brahman needs the mind and senses to enjoy and experience the physical world. However, when the mind is unaware of the master's presence, through lack of discrimination, it is unable to control the senses which run amok like wild horses (3 v.5). Brahman, pure consciousness, is hidden in every heart, being the eternal witness watching everything one does. He is said to be 'the operator' whilst we are his 'innumerable instruments'. (*Svetasvetara Upanishad* 6 v.10-12) When we are ignorant of this Self and identify with the mind (ego), our senses become attached to sense objects, which causes sorrow.

The Gaudiya Vaishnavas say that man's essential nature is spirit, the *Paramatman* existing within each living entity as Vishnu. However, this is clothed, or covered, by the material body (including the senses) and the subtle body of mind, intelligence and false ego.[87] This false ego causes one to identify with the mind and/or body due to ignorance of our true nature. The way to overcome this is to acquire spiritual knowledge by devotion to Krishna, which 'is said to purify our activities because this is transcendental to material conditioning.'[88] The Bhagavad Gita states quite clearly that the soul, or *paramatman*, of each individual is indestructible and that this takes on a new body when the old one dies (2 v.22). Bhaktivedanta regards a human birth

---

[87] A.C. Bhaktivedanta, *Dharma*, 1998, Los Angeles, p.3.
[88] J. Stillson Judah, *Hare Krishna and the Counterculture,* 1974, New York, p.70.

as being particularly auspicious because 'the human body is an excellent vehicle by which we can reach eternal life'.[89]

The Purpose of Life

Advaita Vedanta maintains that the goal or purpose of human life is to become free by realizing the oneness of the *atman*, the apparently individual soul, with Brahman, the Absolute. As Swami Vivekananda says, 'the infinite human soul can never be satisfied but by the Infinite itself.'[90] He decries the seeking of external pleasures, but recommends instead that one realize the truth of one's unity with Brahman, for this leads to bliss (infinite pleasure) as He experiences pleasure through all of the bodies in existence. This realization, he declares, is 'utter freedom and the goal of life.'[91] Many of the Upanishads back this up, some examples being in *Mundaka Upanishad* II Ch.2 v.1, *Katha Upanishad* I Ch.2 v.1, *Kena Upanishad* II v.5, *Svetasvetara Upanishad* II v.14 and *Prasna Upanishad* Q6 v.6.

Gaudiya Vaishnavas, too, believe that the goal of life is to attain liberation or self-realization, which the Srimad Bhagavatam defines as 'surrender by the living entities to Your (Krishna's) control', leading to lasting happiness.[92] By this surrender one is able to realize one's relationship with Krishna (God), which Bhaktivedanta maintains is 'the perfection of life' or Krishna-Consciousness. He states that, as all beings are 'parts and parcel' of God and as the 'parts are meant for

---

[89] A.C. Bhaktivedanta, *The Science of Self Realization,* 1977, Los Angeles, p.5.
[90] Swami Vivekananda, *The Complete Works Vol 4,* 1989, Mayavati, p.240.
[91] Swami Vivekananda, *The Complete Works Vol 2,* 1989, Mayavati, p.469-470.
[92] A.C. Bhaktivedanta, *The Bhagavad Gita As It Is*, 1989, Los Angeles, p.125

serving the whole', we fulfil our purpose by serving Krishna (the whole).[93] He also asserts, quite categorically, that 'the human body is meant for spiritual realization', which the *Srimad Bhagavatam* says can be attained by practicing 'that *Dharma* or religion by which you will advance in unmotivated uninterrupted devotional service to the Lord.'[94]

So although both streams believe that self-realization is the purpose of life, they each have a quite different concept of this. Whereas Advaita Vedanta maintains that this is achieved by realizing the unity of the *atman* with Brahman, the impersonal Absolute, for the Gaudiya Vaishnavas this denotes surrender and devotion to, and realizing one's relationship with Krishna the personal Godhead.

The Afterlife

Advaita Vedanta teaches that the *atman* is immortal and survives death in one of two ways, either by reincarnation or by absorption back into Brahman, the Absolute Reality. Reincarnation occurs when self-realization, or liberation, has not been achieved so that the inner self may 'gain experience and knowledge and achieve liberation'.[95] The *atman* in bondage, which is identified with the mind or body rather than Brahman, is called the *jiva,* which represents the individual soul. It is this which is continually reincarnated until this misidentification ceases and the *atman* realizes its unity with Brahman. After this the *jiva*

---

[93] A.C. Bhaktivedanta, *The Science of Self Realization,* 1977, Los Angeles, p.2-3.
[94] A.C. Bhaktivedanta, *Dharma,* 1998, Los Angeles, p.36.
[95] Swami Ranganathananda, *The Message of the Upanishad s*, 1985, Bombay, p.134.

ceases to exist upon the death of the physical body when the *atman* is absorbed back into Brahman.[96]

The *Brihadaranyaka Upanishad* (VI. Ch2. v.15-16) and the *Chandogya Upanishad* (IV v.15) state that when one dies one either follows the 'northern circuit' on the path of the Gods, which leads through light to merging with Brahman, or the 'southern circuit' which leads through darkness to the world of the ancestors (*pitr-loka*) and from there to rebirth on the earth as a human being or in a lesser form depending on one's *karma*. *Karma* is one's accrued merit, or demerit, generated by one's thoughts and actions from this and previous lives, carried in the subtle body of the *jiva* and which determines the circumstances of one's rebirth.[97]

Gaudiya Vaishnavas also believe in reincarnation for those who have not become self-realized. The soul passes into another body at the time of death. 'The self-realized soul is not bewildered by such a change.' (B.G. Ch.2 v.13) However, this is not because the self-realized soul merges into The Absolute but because these souls go to Goloka-Vrindavan, Krishnaloka the 'supreme planet', where they live for ever in bliss and happiness. This planet is full of 'desire trees' that can grow any food that is desired, beautiful palaces, cows that give limitless milk and is a place where one's desires are all fulfilled. It is also the abode of Krishna where He sports and plays whilst still pervading the entire physical world through his material energy.[98] For

---

[96] Swami Vivekananda, *The Complete Works Vol 2*, 1989, Mayavati, p.314.
[97] Hillary Rodrigues, *Hinduism*, 2006, New York, p.50-51.
[98] J. Stillson Judah, *Hare Krishna and the Counterculture*, 1974, New York, p.57.

those who are not self-realized, or Krishna Conscious, their rebirth is dependent on their *karma*:

> When one dies in the mode of goodness he attains to the pure higher planets. One who dies in the mode of passion takes birth amongst those engaged in frutitive activities and one who dies in the mode of ignorance takes birth in the animal kingdom. (B.G. 14 v.15)

Gaudiya Vaishnavas believe in a spiritual planetary system above and beyond the material universe, containing innumerable planets each ruled by different gods, or demigods, of whom Krishna is supreme. Those who worship other gods, or demigods, go to these planets instead of Krishnaloka, where they reside for a length of time, dependent on their *karma*, before being reborn into the material world.[99] This allows for followers of other spiritual paths to receive their just desserts, but shows that to transcend reincarnation one has to eventually become Krishna Conscious.

Analysis

For the Advaita Vedantist, man is an instrument of Brahman, containing the *atman* which is identical to Brahman. This is the agent, the doer and the experiencer or enjoyer, whilst the mind-body is the instrument through which the *atman* (Brahman) acts in and enjoys His creation. This creation is a manifestation of Brahman, so that the experiencing and enjoying of this divine play is a way for Brahman to know Himself. Once one realizes that one is the *atman*, forever united

---

[99] A.C. Bhaktivedanta, *The Bhagavad Gita As It Is*, 1989, Los Angeles, p.XXX—XXXI.

with Brahman, one is liberated, having attained the purpose of life, and is no longer reborn but merges with Brahman after death. However, if one identifies with the body-mind, the *jiva* which houses the *atman*, one is reincarnated again and again until one realizes the true nature of the self and is liberated.

For the Gaudiya Vaishnavas, man possesses an indestructible soul, the *paramatman*, a partial representation of the Godhead Krishna. This exists eternally as a separate individual entity and remains in a material body as long as it misidentifies with the body, mind, or false ego. The world was created so that these conditioned souls could achieve self-realization and please Krishna through their sacrifices. This self-realization occurs through service of, surrender to and establishing a relationship with Krishna and the attainment of this is the purpose of life. If this is achieved, one goes to Krishnaloka after death, where one lives forever in bliss and happiness with Krishna. However, those who do not become self-realized are born again and again in different realms, depending on their *karma*, until self-realization is achieved.

There are many similarities between the two models but also some fundamental differences. For while both posit that man contains an *atman*, the Advaita Vedantists teach that this is identical to the Absolute; but for the Gaudiya Vaishnavas this *paramatman* is only a facet of this Godhead. Advaita Vedantists teach that this is never separate from the Absolute, whilst Gaudiya Vaishnavas hold that this is always a unique separate entity. So Advaita Vedanta is a nondualistic philosophy, whilst Gaudiya Vaishnavism is essentially dualistic. Both express that the world was created for the Absolute's enjoyment, but for the Advaita Vedantin is an instrument for Brahman to achieve this, whereas for the Gaudiya Vaishnavas this enjoyment is provided by man's actions. Also, both posit that the aim of life is to become self-realized, so as to avoid rebirth and be with the Absolute after death; but while for the Advaita Vedantist this means losing one's self-identity completely and merging with Brahman, for the Gaudiya Vaishnavas this means retaining one's self-identity and living forever in spiritual form with Krishna.

Chapter Five
Buddhism

The Buddhist paths to be considered are Theravadan and Tibetan Buddhism. Theravadan Buddhism is simply denoted by Buddhism as this is the more mainstream of the two. The word Theravada literally means Doctrine of the Elders, which is the doctrine of the Buddha that has been preserved and handed down over the centuries by the Elders, the senior monks.[100] They regard the teachings that they follow to be the direct teachings of the Buddha which were orally transmitted until they were finally written down some hundreds of years later. Tibetan Buddhism is a form of Mahayana Buddhism said to have been taken to Tibet by Padmasambhava in 775AD,[101] where it assimilated some elements of the local animistic Bon religion to form a particular path of its own.

Mahayana Buddhism focuses on 'the Bodhisattva, one on the path to perfect Buddhahood whose task is to compassionately help beings while maturing his or her own wisdom'.[102] Thus the aim of the Mahayana, the great vehicle, is not to achieve *nirvana* as a way to avoid being reborn; rather it is to become enlightened and then strive for the benefit of all beings. This is in contrast to the aim of the Hinayana (a derogatory term coined by the Mahayanists meaning 'the

---

[100] R.F. Gombrich, *Theravada Buddhism*, 1988, London, p.3
[101] P.Harvey, *An Introduction to Buddhism*, 1990, Cambridge, p.145
[102] Ibid, p121.

lesser vehicle'), of which Theravada is the main school, in which the *arhat* escapes from *samsara* – the cyclical wheel of birth, life, death and reincarnation – by achieving *nirvana*. The present Dalai Lama says that Tibetan Buddhism builds on the concepts of Theravadan Buddhism – which it describes as 'the first turning of the wheel of *Dharma*' , or Buddha's early teachings – by focussing on the second turning: The prajnaparamita sutras, purported to have been taught by Buddha towards the end of his life at Vulture's Peak, and which deal with emptiness; and also on the third turning which consists of later teachings dealing with Buddha-Nature.[103]

God

Buddhism has often been described as atheistic, for the Buddha did not talk about the Absolute and refused to answer questions on the subject, instead maintaining a noble silence. This does not necessarily mean that the Buddha denied the existence of an Absolute Reality, but he did deny the existence of an individual self. It appears that he felt that the *atman* (Brahman within each individual) doctrine of Vedanta had been corrupted to the concept of an individual soul or self which exists eternally. So to affirm the existence of the Absolute could have been construed as supporting this doctrine of individual eternalism; but to deny the existence of the Absolute would have supported the doctrine of annihilationism, which would have contradicted the Buddha's own doctrine of *nirvana* (liberation), and thus he chose to

---

[103] The Dalai Lama, *The World of Tibetan Buddhism,* 1995, Boston, p. 15-27

remain silent.[104] However, he is said to have made the following inspired utterance about *nirvana* itself:

> There is, monks, a domain where there is no earth, no water, no wind, no sphere of infinite space, no sphere of neither awareness nor non-awareness; there is not this world, there is not another world, there is no sun or moon. I do not call this coming or going, nor standing, nor dying, nor being reborn; it is without support, without occurrence, without object. Just this is the end of suffering.[105]

This indicates some greater reality which is attained when *nirvana* is reached, but it is described in a totally negative way as being free of all attributes. As Buddhism developed and spread, this idea evolved into the Tibetan (Buddhist) concept of Rigpa or Ground Luminosity and the Zen idea of Universal Mind. Both of these concepts are equivalent to the pure consciousness or awareness in which all appears, exists and disappears. About Rigpa, Sogyal Rinpoche says, 'In Tibetan we call it Rigpa, a primordial, pure, pristine awareness that is at once intelligent, cognizant, radiant and always awake …. It is in fact the nature of everything'.[106] Dudjon Rinpoche adds, 'It has never been born, been liberated, been deluded, existed, been nonexistent, it has no limits and falls into no category'.[107] Padmasambhava, the founder of Tibetan Buddhism in 775AD,[108] described Rigpa as:

---

[104] R.Gethin, *The Foundations of Buddhis'*,1998, Oxford, p. 161
[105] R. Gethin, *Udana 80* in *The Foundations of Buddhism*, 1998, Oxford, p. 76-77
[106] S. Rinpoche *The Tibetan Book of Living and Dying*, 1992, San Francisco, p. 47
[107] Ibid. p. 49
[108] P. Harvey, *Buddhism*, 1990, Cambridge, p. 145

> The self-originated Clear Light which ... was never born. It has never experienced birth and nothing could cause it to die ... although it is evidently visible, yet there is no one who sees it ... Although it exists in everyone everywhere it has gone unrecognized.[109]

According to *The Tibetan Book of the Dead,* Rigpa is the first thing one encounters after death: 'The nature of everything is open, empty and naked like the sky, luminous emptiness without centre or circumference; the pure naked Rigpa dawns'.[110]

Universal or Big Mind is the name used by the Zen school whose 'founding genius was seen as the semi-legendary Indian monk Bodhidharma ... active in China between 470 to 520 AD'.[111] About this Mind he is recorded as saying

> Only the wise know this Mind, this Mind called *dharma* nature, this Mind called liberation. Neither life nor death can restrain this Mind. Nothing can. It's also called the unstoppable *Tathagatha,* the Incomprehensible, the Sacred Self, the Immortal, the Great Sage ... The Mind's capacity is limitless and its manifestations are inexhaustible ... The Mind has no form and its awareness no limit.[112]

---

[109] S. Rinpoche *The Tibetan Book of Living and Dying,* 1992, San Francisco, p. 260
[110] Ibid. p. 259
[111] P. Harvey, '*Buddhism*', 1990, Cambridge, p. 153
[112] S. Rajneesh, '*Bodhidharma*', 1987, Cologne, p. 71-72

We find this Zen Mind also described in *'Zen Mind, Beginner's Mind'* by Shunryu Suzuki as something which is 'always with you', 'watching mind' and 'our true Buddha nature'. He also talks about small 'I' and big 'I' and our 'true self'. Finally, he says, 'You should be able to appreciate things as an expression of Big Mind '. [113]

Creation

Buddhists see existence as infinite in time and space with no known beginning, for however far you go back there must always 'have been a prior cause for whatever existed at that time'.[114] They denote existence by the word *samsara*, 'wandering on', which consists of an endless chain of birth, life, death and rebirth. This applies to world-systems, universes and all beings contained in them, over incalculable eons of time. Within *samsara* there are many realms, the highest being the formless, then the pure-form realms beneath which are the sense-desire realms. Beings in all realms are subject to re-birth, but once one reaches the five pure abodes (of the pure form realm) and higher, then one becomes a 'never-returner and cannot be born in the 'lower realms'.[115]

Buddhists teach that rebirth is to be transcended by achieving *nirvana*, when one goes beyond *samsara*. For although they hold that 'the process of life and rebirth has no inherent purpose, for it was not designed and created by anyone'[116]; they also hold that life is dukkha

---

[113] S. Suzuki, 'Zen Mind, Beginners' Mind', 1970, New York, p. 134-137
[114] P.Harvey, *An Introduction to Buddhism*, 1990, Cambridge, p.32
[115] P.Williams, *Buddhist Thought,* 2000, London, p. 77-78

or suffering, and that the process of death and rebirth is unpleasant. In fact, Buddha's most essential teaching, The Four Noble Truths, deals directly with this suffering, its cause and its remedy. This remedy results in *nirvana*, liberation, which can be achieved directly from the human realm, for 'this is a matter of gnosis which could in theory be obtained anywhere and at anytime'.[117] Buddhist tradition holds that those realms below the human are not conducive to this gnosis occurring. In contrast to this, Nagarjuna, the originator of Mahayana Buddhism, of which Tibetan Buddhism is one stream, maintained that the World is to be transcended not because of its pain and sorrow, but because it is as non-real as are dreams and thus totally unsatisfactory.

Nagarjuna maintained that behind *samsara* is the True Universal Essence which is composed of three aspects known as the Tri-Kaya, or three worlds.[118] These are the Dharmakaya, 'the dimension of empty unconditioned Truth', the Sambhogakaya, 'the dimension of complete enjoyment' and the Nirmanakaya, 'the dimension of ceaseless manifestation.'[119] These are also known as the three bodies of the Buddha, Nirmanakaya representing the earthly Buddhas, Sambhogakaya representing the Buddhas in their heavens and Dharmakaya representing Buddha-Nature or *Shunyata* (the Void).

In Tibetan Buddhism, Nirmanakaya can represent the 'intentional embodiment of a reborn master', whilst Sambhogakaya can refer 'to the means of achieving the Dharmakaya by meditation on the various

---

[116] P.Harvey, *An Introduction to Buddhism*, 1990, Cambridge, p.38
[117] P.Williams, *Buddhist Thought*, 2000, London, p. 78
[118] W.Y. Evans-Wentz, *The Tibetan Book of Great Liberation*, 2000, New York, p.3
[119] S. Rinpoche, *The Tibetan Book of Living and Dying*, 1992, San Francisco, p. 343

visualised deities called *gidams* which are archetypal symbols'.[120] They can also refer to the body, speech and mind of a master, being represented by the *mudra,* the *mantra* and the *mandala.* Sogyal Rinpoche describes these as three aspects of Rigpa, the 'Ground Luminosity' or 'Universal Essence', representing 'its empty sky-like essence' (Dharmakaya), 'its radiant luminous nature' (Sambhogakaya) and 'its compassionate energy' (Nirmanakaya), which are all 'simultaneously present and interpenetrating as one.'[121]

The Nature of Man

With regard to self-identity, Buddhists maintain that there is no eternal self, soul, or *atman,* a theory they call *anatta,* which literally means 'no *atman*'. They regard persons as being a combination of physical material form and mental states of feeling, perception, disposition (intentions/volitions) and consciousness. These five are known as the bundle of aggregates (*kandhas*), each of which combines with the others in a dynamic bundle. This bundle exists moment to moment, with each bundle-moment causing the following bundle-moment. Thus the impression of the continuity of a person is given by a series of instantaneous causally linked person stages (bundle-moments) flowing into each other. At death it is claimed that the bundle of aggregates, except the material form, reconfigures in accordance with *karmic* causation, unless the person has attained *nirvana*, in which case no re-birth occurs. The new bundle is then reborn into a material form and

---

[120] C. George Boeree, *Buddhist Cosmology*, http://webspace.ship.edu/cgboer/buddhacosmo.html
[121] S. Rinpoche, *The Tibetan Book of Living and Dying*, 1992, San Francisco, p. 343

circumstances commensurate with the *karmic* residue of the previous bundle. Thus the Buddhists deny that there is any sort of persisting entity that continues over time. A person appears to exist and continue as a separate entity, but this is an illusion. Just as a river is not in fact a single entity but a continuous flow of water, so a person is a flow of causally linked person stages or bundle-moments.[122]

Mahayana and Tibetan Buddhism have expanded the concept of *anatta* to that of emptiness, *Shunyata*:

> Early Buddhism, with its teaching on not-self, or *Anatta*, taught that there is no such thing as an enduring self or soul... As Buddhism developed, the *Anatta* doctrine was subsumed into something more extensive in which all phenomena were seen to be 'empty' of self or essence.[123]

This means that literally everything is empty, like a magical illusion. Or, to put another way, everything is a 'conceptual construct and has no own-existence, empty of individual primary irreducible existence'.[124] This corresponds with the string theory which says everything is composed of strings of energy vibrating at different frequencies, thus nothing has any intrinsic irreducible existence. The present Dalai Lama states that 'all phenomena are empty and selfless' and maintains that this understanding is much more powerful than the mere recognition of *anatta*, no-self. This is because this counters the delusion that phenomena are inherently existent, thus enabling one to 'overcome the subtle clinging to external objects'.[125] When everything is realized to be

---

[122] P.Harvey, *An Introduction to Buddhism*, 1990, Cambridge, p.49-50
[123] www.buddhism.about.com/6/a/2003_12_03
[124] P. Williams, *Buddhist Thought*, 2000, London, p.134-135
[125] The Dalai Lama, *The World of Tibetan Buddhism*, 1995, Boston, p. 31-34

intrinsically empty then all grasping and attachment cease, for there is ultimately no one to grasp and nothing to grasp for or to be attached to.

The Purpose of Life

Buddhism maintains that the main purpose of life is to overcome suffering. The Buddha stated that, 'One thing I teach is suffering and the end of suffering. It is just ill and the ceasing of that ill that I proclaim'.[126] His primary teaching to achieve this was the Four Noble Truths (suffering, its cause, that it can be overcome and how to do this), described as 'the most fundamental and basic teaching of Buddhism'.[127] The cause of suffering is craving and clinging, which has many aspects one of which is the sense of self-attachment, that is, attaching to 'phenomena or sense objects as self or as belonging to self'.[128] To overcome this, Buddha suggested the Eightfold Path which centres on the concepts of *anatta*, no-self and *anicca*, the impermanence of all things. Once one has realized that there is no essential self and that all things are ephemeral and impermanent then there is truly no one to crave and nothing which is permanent to which to cling.

The Dalai Lama has stated unequivocally that, 'I believe the purpose of life is to be happy'. Whilst this is to be achieved by overcoming one's own suffering through reaching *nirvana*, in Mahayana Buddhism the

---

[126] www.religionfacts.com/buddhism/beliefs/purpose.htm
[127] M. Choong, *RELS305/405 Buddhism: A History, Lecture Notes*, 2004, Armidale, p.11
[128] M. Choong, *RELS305/405 Buddhism: A History, Lecture Notes*, 2004, Armidale, p.12

emphasis is upon developing love and compassion for one's fellow beings. For as he said,

> From my own limited experience I have found that the greatest degree of inner tranquility comes from the development of love and compassion. The more we care for the happiness of others, the greater our own sense of well-being becomes... It is the ultimate source of success in life. [129]

The gaining of compassion could be called a secondary purpose, which ties in with the Bodhisattva ideal of becoming enlightened so as to strive for the benefit of all beings, rather than for escaping from *samsara*.

Sogyal Rinpoche maintains that the practice of compassion is the most powerful way of overcoming self-grasping and self-cherishing, thus overcoming our attachment to a non-existent self. Compassion is not only to be practiced after enlightenment, but is in itself a powerful tool to aid in achieving this enlightenment. In fact he goes so far as to describe it as 'the source and essence of enlightenment'.[130]

Chogyam Trungpa talks of compassion as being open and generous, without any direction, or a 'me' and 'others'. He says that it is filled with joy, wealth and richness which you can share with others, thus generating more joy, wealth and richness and so on. He calls this the 'open way' where you learn to trust your own fundamental richness and thus live spontaneously without fear. He says that this generosity and

---

[129] http://buddhism.kalachakranet.org/resources/purpose_life_dalai_lama.html
[130] S. Rinpoche, *The Tibetan Book of Living and Dying*, 1992, San Francisco, p. 188-189

openness is the start of the Bodhisattva Path, which is the surrendering of a false notion of self and others.[131]

The Afterlife

As previously stated, Buddhism teaches the *samsaric* cycle of birth, death and rebirth until one achieves *nirvana*. Buddhists are taught that the circumstances of one's life and rebirth are determined by one's *karma*, the accumulated merit/demerit stored up by one's previous thoughts and actions. The *Dhammapada* says,

> Those who are selfish suffer in this life and the next. They suffer seeing the results of the evil they have done and more suffering awaits them in the next life. But those who are selfless rejoice in this life and the next. They rejoice seeing the deeds they have done and more joy awaits them in the next life. (Ch1 v.17-18)[132]

"Selfless' and 'Selfish' can mean the difference between recognizing and not recognizing the truth of *anatta,* and can also mean the usual definitions of being generous or grasping.

Theravadan Buddhists have a unique doctrine of *bhavanga*, which means 'an inactive level of mind which is still present when no mental activity is occurring'. This is directly transferred from the dying person, at the moment of death, to the embryo of its new body as it experiences its first arising of consciousness, and so this *bhavanga* is

---

[131]Chogyam Trungpa, *Cutting through Spiritual Materialism*, 1987, London, p. 98-100
[132]Easwaran E., *The Dhammapada, verses 17-1,'* 1986, Petaluma, p. 80

the causal link between the two. Therefore, Theravadan Buddhists do not believe in any intermediate state between death and rebirth.[133]

There is also the belief that the death-thought is a special form of *bhavanga*, which is of great importance in determining the circumstances of one's subsequent rebirth. In the Theravadan Pathavattu and Vimanavattu, there are stories of monks visiting dying lay followers to ensure they maintain wholesome thoughts and 'the Buddha recommends that lay followers similarly encourage one another in Buddhist virtues on such occasions.'[134]

Tibetan Buddhists believe in *bardos*, intermediate stages between death and rebirth. *Bardo* literally means 'suspended in between' and Sogyal Rinpoche divides the whole of existence into four *bardos*: the 'natural' *bardo* of this life, the 'painful' *bardo* of dying, the 'luminous' *bardo* of *Dharma*datta and the '*karmic*' *bardo* of becoming. The first is 'in between' birth and the commencement of death; the second is 'in between' the start of the dying process and the 'dawning of the nature of mind…Ground Luminosity'; the third is 'in between' the moment of death and the passing of the Ground Luminosity; and the fourth is 'in between' this passing and the moment of rebirth.[135]

At death one enters the Ground Luminosity which represents our inherent buddha-nature. If one is able to recognize this, one is liberated and freed from *samsara* and rebirth. However, most people shy away

---

[133] P. Williams, *Buddhist Thought*, 2000, London, p. 123
[134] S. Collins, *Selfless Persons*, 1982, Cambridge, p. 244-245
[135] S. Rinpoche, *The Tibetan Book of Living and Dying*, 1992, San Francisco, p. 102-104

from this due to ignorance and pass into the *karmic bardo*. About this Padmasambhava said:

> All beings have lived died and been reborn countless times. Over and over again they have experienced the indescribable Clear Light (Ground Luminosity). But because they are obscured by the darkness of ignorance they wander endlessly in limitless *samsara*.[136]

This *bardo* lasts, on average, forty-nine days whilst waiting to establish a *karmic* connection to our future parents. During this time one goes through many experiences: not realizing one is dead and trying to communicate with loved ones; reliving the experiences of one's past lives; re-experiencing dying; and wandering through *karmic* mind-created realms of varying pleasure and horror. Finally one arrives at the union of one's next parents and enters the newly conceived embryo.[137]

Analysis

With regard to considering the correlation between world-view and self-identity, this is particularly tricky because Buddhists would agree that no separate essential self exists. Therefore the correlation, or mutual relationship, between these concepts is that between 'something' and 'nothing'! However, this nothingness is not only what Buddhists believe we actually are, but it is also that which Buddhists aim to realize by achieving *nirvana*, or recognizing and merging with the clear light. For *nirvana* was described by the Buddha in terms of a 'domain of

---

[136] *Ibid,* p. 260-261
[137] *Ibid,* p. 289-291

nothingness... (which is) the end of suffering', and the 'clear light' (Rigpa) was described in the Tibetan Book of the Dead as 'luminous emptiness'.

Thus, although creation, *samsara*, is without purpose, there is a method of escaping from this wheel of birth and death by achieving *nirvana* or recognizing the clear light. Buddhists believe that this is advisable as life is *dukkha* (suffering), whilst Tibetan Buddhists would go even further describing life as unreal as a dream and thus totally unsatisfactory. This escape from *samsara* therefore becomes the purpose of life for Theravadan Buddhists, and whilst Tibetan Buddhists would ultimately agree with this, they maintain that one should eschew the final *nirvana*, or blowing out of the candle, and selflessly help others until all are liberated.

Although humans have no essential self, Buddhists are taught that, for those who are not liberated, when the physical body dies the bundle of the four mental *kandhas* reconfigures in accordance with *karmic* causation. Whilst the process of this reconfiguration is seen differently in Theravadan and Tibetan Buddhism, they both believe that the new bundle is then reborn into a material form and circumstances, commensurate with the *karmic* residue of the previous bundle. So although we have no inherent intrinsic self-identity, there is continuity of an apparent self until this fact is fully realized. In the final analysis the Buddhist world-view is that the world is a place to be transcended and this is to be done by realizing the truths of *anatta* (no self) and *anicca* (impermanence), in Theravadan Buddhism, or the truth of *Shunyata* (emptiness) in Mahayana Buddhism. Once one has fully realized this then there is truly 'no self' and no one who needs to escape *samsara* or achieve *nirvana*.

Chapter Six

Ramakrishna – A Living Example

This chapter is about the Indian saint and mystic Sri Ramakrishna, who is chosen to highlight the themes explored earlier. Such was his spiritual aptitude that it enabled him to reach the zenith, the culmination, in an amazingly short time, of any practice to which he turned his mind and being. Whereas most mystics struggle along a single path for a whole, some would say more than one, lifetime, often without reaching the ultimate experience obtainable, Sri Ramakrishna was able to complete every path that he tried in less than six months. This makes him particularly useful to study as he followed four of the ten paths previously considered; almost anyone else that could have been chosen would have only followed one.

The four paths in question are Vaishnavism (the worship of any form of Vishnu), Advaita Vedanta (Absolute nondualism), Islam and Christianity. He also mastered many other Hindu spiritual practices and, on the completion of his many *sadhanas* or spiritual practices, he gathered many devotees from a wide variety of spiritual paths, whom he was able to instruct on their own particular path. Through this process he was exposed to Buddhism and, although he did not practice this as a spiritual path, he was able to bring his wealth of experience to bear when considering the Buddha and his teachings.

This chapter starts with a short spiritual biography which introduces the reader to Sri Ramakrishna, thus enabling one a deeper appreciation of the more detailed material that follows. This highlights the many spiritual practices that he completed before becoming a teacher in his own right. Next, the four *sadhanas*, which are particularly relevant to the thesis, are considered in turn.

The main source used is *The Gospel of Ramakrishna*, a hagiography covering the period between 1882 and 1887, composed by Mahendranath Gupta who was a headmaster at a local school. During this period he visited Ramakrishna many times and on each visit he described the scene, the events and faithfully recorded every word said by and to Ramakrishna. This makes it an invaluable resource. Over 1000 pages, it contains many utterances by Ramakrishna on just about every spiritual topic imaginable. In the introduction there is a succinct, detailed biography of Ramakrishna which was extremely useful in preparing the section on his spiritual life.

One other point before consideration of the spiritual life of Sri Ramakrishna is that this is not a critical assessment but a comparison between Ramakrishna's world-view, which includes his sense of self-identity, and the world-view of those paths which he followed, mentioned earlier in this book. His experiences and views are not subjected to any kind of critical or rational analysis. This is because his experiences and interpretation of these formed his world-view and sense of self-identity and are independent of any views of these that an external commentator may have. What follows is based entirely on his accounts of his experiences, those which he shared with his devotees and reminiscences of those that knew him. This implies that the reader must suspend all personal judgements and disbelief and accept the account of his spiritual life and experiences at face value. This rider has been added, for what follows may seem somewhat strange to the Western rational mind and indeed to anyone who does not have a fairly extensive knowledge of Hinduism and its various paths to God-realization.

The Spiritual Life of Sri Ramakrishna

Ramakrishna was born in 1836, in the small rural village of Karmakupur, in the Hooghly district of Bengal. This location was one of idyllic simplicity, untouched by any form of modernity, as it was far from the railway and the city. His parents were devout Vaishnavas, being devotees of Rama, one of the incarnations of Vishnu, who was their family deity and worshipped daily in their home. In 1835 his father, Khudiram, visited the holy shrine at Gaya, said to contain the footprint of Lord Vishnu. Whilst there he had a vision of a luminous person, Vishnu, who being very pleased with his sincere devotion, promised to be born as his son 'to chastise the wicked and protect the virtuous'.[138] Meanwhile his mother, Chandra Devi, was having visions of a luminous figure lying beside her and then of a flood of light issuing from a Shiva *lingam* and entering her body.[139] These events presaged the birth of Ramakrishna who was named Gadadhar, an epithet for Vishnu, in honour of his father's vision at Gaya.

---

[138] S. Ananyananda, *Life of Sri Ramakrishna*, 1983, Mayavati, p.8
[139] *Ibid* p.8-9

Gadadhar grew up to be a fun-filled, healthy, precocious child with a prodigious memory, whose main delight was to listen to stories about Gods and Goddesses from Hindu mythology and the epics. He loved to mould images of these divine beings out of clay and to lead his classmates in staging dramas based on stories from the *Ramayana* and the *Mahabharata*. At the age of six or seven he had his first mystical experience when, being overwhelmed by the beauty of a flight of snow-white cranes against the backdrop of a dark thunder cloud, he fell to the ground in a state of indescribable joy and had to be carried home.[140]

When he was seven his father died and, realizing the impermanence of life, he began to spend many hours in meditation in the nearby mango orchard or at the local cremation grounds. He also spent much time with the many holy men who passed through Karmakupur on their way to Puri. At the age of nine he was invested with the sacred thread, which gave him the privileges of his Brahmin lineage and allowed him to perform the worship of his family deity, Raghuvir (Ramachandra or Sri Rama).[141] Thus Gadadhar lived in rural simplicity and deep spiritual practice until he was sixteen, when he was summoned to Calcutta to assist his elder brother, Ramkumar, in his priestly duties.

In 1855 a rich widow, Rani Rasmani, needed a Brahmin priest for a large Kali temple that she had commissioned at Dakshineswar, on the

---

[140] The Gospel of Ramakrishna, tr by Sw. Nikhilananda,1942, Ramakrishna-Vivekananda Centre, New York, p.4
[141] *Ibid* p.5

banks of the Ganges. Ramkumar was appointed the priest of the Kali temple and shortly afterwards Ramakrishna, as Gadadhar came to be known, accepted the position of priest in the Radhakanta temple. Then in 1856 Ramkumar died, which resulted in the elevation of Ramakrishna to the priest of the Kali temple and propelled him along the path to God-realization.

Kali, the Divine Mother, represents the power of Brahman or *Sakti*, the totality of cosmic energy. Brahman, pure cosmic consciousness, has two aspects: the first is the witnessing aspect of pure awareness, consciousness when totally at rest, represented by Shiva; the second is the aspect of creation, preservation and destruction, consciousness in motion (energy), represented by *Sakti* or Kali.[142] Everything in manifestation is composed of *Sakti*, cosmic energy, which appears in, exists in and disappears back into pure awareness, Shiva. Therefore anything in existence can be worshipped as a manifestation of Kali, the Divine Mother.

Ramakrishna totally immersed himself in the worship of Kali and, when not in the temple engaged in this, would meditate in a deep jungle to the north of the compound. His yearning for a vision of the Mother was so great that he could not bear to be without a vision of her and he finally picked up the sword in the Kali temple, determined to end his life. At that point 'the blessed Mother revealed Herself ... everything vanished from sight leaving a limitless, infinite, effulgent Ocean of Consciousness.'[143]

---

[142] *Ibid* p.6-13
[143] *Ibid* p.14

From then on he lived in a totally God-intoxicated state from which sprang the desire to worship and experience God in as many ways as possible. He spent some time imitating Hanuman, the monkey chieftain devotee of Rama. He lived on fruits and roots, wore his dhoti swinging between his legs like a tail and jumped from place to place. After a short time he had a vision of Sita, the consort of Rama, who merged with his body saying 'I bequeath you my smile'.[144]

His next *sadhana* was initiated by the Brahmani, a fifty year old nun who was an adept in Tantra and Vaishnava methods of worship. After studying him for sometime she openly declared that he, like Sri Chaitanya, was an incarnation of God, an *avatar*. Ramakrishna was determined to learn all he could from her and decided to practice the disciplines of the Tantra, with her as his guru. The aim of Tantra is 'to sublimate *bhoga* (enjoyment) into yoga, union with Consciousness'[145] by regarding all women as the embodiment of Kali and practising rites requiring members of the opposite sex. Ramakrishna, under the guidance of the Brahmani, practised all of the disciplines of the sixty-four principal Tantric books, achieving the desired result of each one in less than three days. He had many wonderful visions and experiences, including the full awakening of the Kundalini, accompanied by its passage from the lowest *chakra* through the Shushumna canal to the Sahasrara, the thousand petal lotus in the top of the head. This experience is the culmination of all the Tantric disciplines.[146]

---

[144] *Ibid* p.16
[145] *Ibid* p.21
[146] *Ibid* p.22

Next he was guided by the Brahmani in various forms of Vaishnavic worship, through love of and devotion to Vishnu in his various incarnations. Vaishnavism is exclusively a religion of *bhakti*, devotion, in which one may adopt five different approaches, or attitudes, towards God. Ramakrishna explained these as:

> *Santa,* the serene attitude... It is like the devotion of a wife to her husband.
> *Dasya,* the attitude of a servant towards his master. Hanuman had this attitude towards Rama.
> *Sakhya,* the attitude of friendship.
> *Vatsalya,* the attitude of a mother towards her child. This was Yasoda's attitude towards Krishna.
> *Madhur,* the attitude of a woman towards her paramour. Radha had this towards Krishna. The wife also feels it for her husband. This attitude includes the other four.[147]

Ramakrishna had already completed the first three approaches during his worship of Raghuvir and by his assuming the attitude of Hanuman when worshipping Rama. His chance came to adopt the fourth attitude, that of a mother towards her child, when a wandering Vaishnava monk, Jatadhari, arrived at Dakshineswar temple accompanied by Ramlala, a small metal image of the boy Rama. The image had become a living presence for Jatadhari after many years of devotion and spiritual practice. He devoted himself to feeding, nursing, bathing, caring for and playing with Ramlala and for him the image responded to his love. Ramakrishna soon developed a strong bond with Ramlala, for whom he developed motherly love, to the point where his speech and gestures became feminine and he began to regard himself as a woman. For him Ramlala would dance gracefully, jump on his back,

---

[147] *Ibid* p.115

insist on being cuddled, run in the fields and play naughty pranks like a young child. Through this worship he had a vision of Rama whereby

> He realized that Rama pervades the whole universe as Spirit and Consciousness; that is He is its Creator, Sustainer and Destroyer; that, in still another aspect, He is the transcendental Brahman, without form, attribute or name.[148]

Next he adopted the attitude of *madhur*, in which he regarded himself as one of the gopis of Vrindavan, longing for union with the beloved Krishna. He dressed as a woman and spent many days weeping and imploring Krishna to appear, which He did but only fleetingly and distantly. Finally he turned to praying to Radha for her help and shortly she appeared and he felt her merge with his own body. So now he worshipped Krishna as Radha, His divine consort, and he experienced *mahabhava*, the greatest ecstatic love possible. Shortly afterwards he was granted the resplendent vision of Sri Krishna, who also merged with him. With this he became oblivious to the world, seeing only Krishna in himself and the universe; thus he experienced immortal bliss and 'attained the fulfilment of the worship of the Personal God'.[149]

Following this he was initiated into Advaita Vedanta (nondualism) by Totapuri, a wandering naked ascetic who had realized his unity with Brahman. According to this philosophy only Brahman is real, all else is illusion, *Maya*. Brahman is beyond time, space, causality and multiplicity and can be realized by 'piercing the veil of *Maya* and discovering one's identity with Brahman'.[150] Totapuri advised

---

[148] *Ibid* p.24
[149] *Ibid* p.25
[150] *Ibid* p.26

Ramakrishna to withdraw his mind from the external world and concentrate on Brahman, the Absolute. He had no difficulty transcending the objects of the material world, but then the radiant form of the Divine Mother always appeared and however hard he tried he could go no further than this and he finally despaired telling Totapuri that the endeavour was hopeless. At this Totapuri excitedly picked up a piece of broken glass and, thrusting this into Ramakrishna's eyebrow centre, he told him to concentrate on that. This time, when the image of the Divine Mother appeared, Ramakrishna used his 'discrimination as a sword and with it clove her in two'.[151] Thus he achieved union with Brahman and remained in *nirvikalpa samadhi* for three days. This is the highest state of absorption in the Absolute achievable, in which all contact with the exterior world ceases and all sense of duality disappears.[152] About the realization that this imparted Ramakrishna said,

> When I think of the Supreme Being as inactive, neither creating, nor preserving, nor destroying, I call him Brahman or Purusha, the Impersonal God. When I think of Him as active, creating, preserving and destroying, I call him *Sakti* or *Maya*, the Personal God. But the distinction between them does not mean a difference. The Personal and the Impersonal are the same thing, like milk and its whiteness, the diamond and its lustre, the snake and its wriggling motion. It is impossible to conceive of one without the other. The Divine Mother and Brahman are one.[153]

When Totapuri left Dakshineswar, Ramakrishna remained in the inert state of union with Brahman for six months. He would not have survived had it not been for the attentions of a kindly monk who would

---

[151] *Ibid* p.29
[152] B. Usha, *A Ramakrishna Vedanta Wordbook*, 1971, Hollywood, p.52
[153] *Ibid* p.32

force morsels of food into Ramakrishna's mouth, as soon as he detected the slightest flickering of consciousness.

After this, many wandering holy men and devotees were attracted to Ramakrishna, delighted by his knowledge, his company and his God intoxication. By his experience in many Hindu paths he was able to guide devotees along their own chosen path. During this time he came into contact with and practiced Christianity and Islam, resulting in him experiencing visions of Christ and Muhammad, followed by absorption in *samadhi*. These *sadhanas* are discussed in more detail in a later section.

Although Ramakrishna was capable of achieving *nirvikalpa samadhi* at will, his love of Kali and his devotees, kept him in the world. He often said that the Divine Mother had commanded him to stay at a slightly lower level so that he could teach and interact with his devotees and also so that he could worship Her. In fact, he so much enjoyed the company of his devotees and his God intoxicated states, that when he felt *nirvikalpa samadhi* was immanent he would often avoid dropping into it by banging himself on top of the head.

Ramakrishna and Vaishnavism

This section compares the views of the Gaudiya Vaishnavas, enunciated in the chapter on Hinduism, and those of Ramakrishna in his Vaishnavic attitude. The five elements of world-view used in the thesis are: the nature of God, the nature and purpose of the creation, the essential nature of a human being, the purpose of life and the afterlife. This comparison considers each of these elements in turn.

God

Vaishnavas do not view God as an impersonal Absolute, but as a supreme personality with whom human beings can and should build a personal relationship. The two most common incarnations of Vishnu that are worshipped, in this regard, are Rama and Krishna, both of whom Ramakrishna worshipped devoutly and eagerly. In fact his very name gives the clue to this and he was commonly regarded to be such an incarnation in his own right. He confirmed his opinion of this when, on his own deathbed, he told Vivekananda, his chief disciple, that 'He who was Rama and Krishna is now, in this body Ramakrishna – but not in your Vedantic sense'.[154]

This indicated that he believed that there was some 'supercharged personal divine essence' that is reborn again and again in different forms, which is in accord with his father's vision of Vishnu who said, 'I am born again and again to chastise the wicked and protect the virtuous.'[155] This is also stated in the Bhagavad Gita: 'I am born in every age to protect the good, to destroy evil and to re-establish Dharma.' (Chapter 4 v.8).[156] However, he was not in total agreement

---

[154] *Ibid* p.72
[155] Sw. Ananyananda, *Life of Sri Ramakrishna*, 1983, Mayavati, p.8
[156] E. Easwaran, *The End of Sorrow*, 1983, Petaluma, p.222

with the Gaudiya Vaishnavas who believe that Krishna is the Absolute Truth, whilst the impersonal Brahman represents the glow or effulgence of this Godhead.[157] Ramakrishna turned this around when he said that there are two aspects of Krishna which are 'like the sun and its rays. The Absolute may be likened to the sun and the Relative to the rays.'[158] He also described Rama as 'both Brahman Absolute and a perfect incarnation of God in human form.'[159] So he regarded the Relative, the incarnation, as the rays (or effulgence) of the Absolute Brahman, which is the reverse of the Gaudiya Vaishnava position.

Creation

Gaudiya Vaishnavas believe in cyclical creation with each cycle being a 'breath of Vishnu' which last four billion three hundred million years.[160] They also maintain that Krishna created the material world using his inferior energy which, according to Chaitanya's philosophy of *bhedabheda,* is different from Krishna, who is unaffected by it.[161] Ramakrishna also believed in cyclical creation, which is carried out by the power of *Sakti*, the Divine Mother, about which he said,

> After the destruction of the universe, at the end of a great cycle, my Divine Mother, the embodiment of Brahman, gathers together the seeds for the next creation. After the creation the Primal Power dwells in the universe itself… God is the container of the universe and also what is contained in it.[162]

---

[157] A.C. Bhaktivedanta, *Dharma*, 1998, Los Angeles, p43-45.
[158] The Gospel of Ramakrishna, tr by Sw. Nikhilananda,1942, Ramakrishna-Vivekananda Centre, New York, p.920
[159] *Ibid* p.189
[160] J. Stillson Judah, *Hare Krishna and the Counterculture,* 1974, New York, p.57
[161] *Ibid* p.55
[162] The Gospel of Ramakrishna, tr by Sw. Nikhilananda,1942, Ramakrishna-

This material universe, the Relative, can also be ascribed to Krishna, for according to the *Devi Purana*, Kali Herself has become Krishna. However, according to another *Purana*, Krishna himself is the Absolute, whilst Radha (his consort) is its Divine Power. About this Ramakrishna said, 'what difference does it make? God is infinite and infinite are the ways to reach Him'.[163] Explaining this further he said that,

> An incarnation of God is for the sake of the *bhakta*s (those on the path of devotion) and not for the jnanis (those on the path of knowledge). It is said in the *Adhayatma Ramayana* that Rama alone is both the Pervading Spirit (the Absolute) and everything pervaded (the Relative).[164]

Thus Rama and Krishna are both epithets for Brahman who creates and pervades the universe, However, a 'supercharged personal essence' of Brahman incarnates for the sake of the *bhakta*s. Ramakrishna used to compare Brahman to an ocean with blocks of ice floating in it which represent personal forms of God and His incarnations. Thus these personal forms are of the same substance as Brahman, but appear in various different physical manifestations.[165]

The Nature of Man

Vivekananda Centre, New York, p.135
[163] *Ibid* p.505-6
[164] *Ibid* p.789
[165] H. Torwesten, *Ramakrishna and Christ*, Calcutta, 1999, p.18

Gaudiya Vaishnavas regard man's essential nature as spirit, the *paramatman* existing within each being as Vishnu, which is clothed or covered by the material body and the subtle body of mind, intelligence and false ego.[166] This *paramatman* is regarded as indestructible, travelling from body to body, but forever separate from Krishna. For one of the main purposes of life is to remain an eternal devotee of Krishna, finally residing with Him in Krishnaloka, the 'supreme planet' where one lives for ever in bliss and happiness.[167] Ramakrishna, who had himself experienced union with Krishna, disagreed with this:

> There are three classes of devotee. The lowest one says 'God is up there'. That is he points to heaven. The mediocre devotee says that God dwells in the heart as the 'Inner Controller'. But the highest devotee says that 'God alone has become everything. All that we perceive are so many forms of God'.[168]

For he knew by his experience of absorption with Brahman that the essential nature of man, the *atman*, is not separate from Brahman who has indeed become everything. However, he also said that the devotee keeps a trace of ego so that he may enjoy God, as divine bliss can only be experienced when one makes a distinction between oneself and God.[169] For once one merges with the Absolute (Brahman), all experience ceases, even if bliss is present there is no one separate to experience this. In this state, *nirvikalpa samadhi*, all contact with the external world is lost, including that of thoughts and sensations and thus no experience is possible. Thus the *bhakta*, the devotee, prefers to remain separate so as to experience the bliss of the Personal God.

---

[166] A.C. Bhaktivedanta, *Dharma*, 1998, Los Angeles, p.3.
[167] J. Stillson Judah, *Hare Krishna and the Counterculture,* 1974, New York, p.57.
[168] The Gospel of Ramakrishna, tr by Sw. Nikhilananda,1942, Ramakrishna-Vivekananda Centre, New York, p.396
[169] *Ibid,* p.678

The ultimate realization attainable on this path is known as *savikalpa Samadhi*...

> the first stage of transcendental consciousness, in which the distinction between subject and object persists. In this state the spiritual aspirant may have a vision of the Personal God, with or without form.[170]

Indeed all of the five attitudes of Vaishnavic worship are those of developing personal relationships with one's chosen ideal or form of Vishnu, so that one may experience communion with that chosen ideal.

The Purpose of Life

Gaudiya Vaishnavas believe that the goal or purpose of life is to attain liberation or self-realization, which the Srimad Bhagavatam defines as 'surrender by the living entities to Your (Krishna's) control' and this will make one happy[171]. By this surrender one is able to realize one's relationship with Krishna (God), which Bhaktivedanta maintains is 'the perfection of life' or Krishna-Consciousness. The life of Ramakrishna demonstrates the importance he placed upon developing his relationship with God, in many different modes, both with and without form. Herein lies the major difference between Ramakrishna and the Gaudiya Vaishnavas, or any other sect of any religion; whereas they all stress that their way or deity is the best or only way (or deity), Ramakrishna made no distinction, trying as many ways and approaching God in as many modes as possible. Whilst he was totally convinced that the purpose of life was to realize God, he would not

---

[170] B. Usha, *A Ramakrishna Vedanta Wordbook*, 1971, Hollywood, p.70
[171] A.C. Bhaktivedanta, *The Bhagavad Gita As It Is*, 1989, Los Angeles, p.125

have dreamed of limiting this to Krishna, Rama, Shiva , Brahman, Jehovah, Allah or any other name or form of God. For by his experience he knew that these are just different names and forms of the one Absolute Reality which manifests in various modes, both of form and of formlessness, and may be approached in many different ways.

The Afterlife

After death, Gaudiya Vaishnavas believe in reincarnation for those who have not become self-realized:

> As the same person inhabits the body through childhood, youth and old age, so too at the time of death he attains another body. The man of wisdom is not deluded by these changes. (Bhagavad Gita Ch.2 v.13)[172]

For those who are not Krishna Conscious, their rebirth is dependent on their *karma*, which is one's accrued merit, or demerit, generated by one's thoughts and actions, from this and previous lives, carried in the subtle body from life to life.[173] Those who have achieved realization go to Goloka-Vrindavan, Krishnaloka, the supreme planet, where they live for ever in bliss and happiness. This planet is full of 'desire trees' that can grow any food that is desired, beautiful palaces, cows that give limitless milk and is a place where one's desires are all fulfilled. It is also the abode of Krishna, in form, where He sports and plays whilst still pervading the entire physical world through his material energy.[174]

---

[172] E. Easwaran, *The End of Sorrow,* 1983, Petaluma, p.61
[173] Hillary Rodrigues, *Hinduism*, 2006, New York, p.50-51.
[174] J. Stillson Judah, *Hare Krishna and the Counterculture,* 1974, New York, p.57.

When asked what happens after death, Ramakrishna also relied on the Bhagavad Gita:

> According to the Gita one becomes afterwards what one thinks of at the time of death. King Bharata thought of his deer and became a deer in his next life. Therefore one must practice *sadhana* in order to realize God. If a man thinks of God day and night, he will have the same thought in the hour of death.[175]

He maintained that for those who have realized God there is no rebirth, they are totally liberated and 'do not go to another plane of existence'.[176] However, Ramakrishna discouraged speculation about what occurs after death, stressing that one should enjoy living in devotion to God, rather than calculating about the afterlife.

Ramakrishna and Advaita Vedanta

This section compares the views of Advaita Vedanta and Ramakrishna concerning the five elements of world-view: the nature of God, the nature and purpose of the creation, the essential nature of a human being, the purpose of life and the afterlife.

God

Advaita Vedanta regards the Absolute, Brahman, as the only 'thing' in existence. This is the source, creator, container, destroyer and

---

[175] The Gospel of Ramakrishna, tr by Sw. Nikhilananda,1942, Ramakrishna-Vivekananda Centre, New York, p.583
[176] *Ibid*, p.668

essence of everything in manifestation; thus everything in existence is nothing but Brahman Itself. Everything appears through *Maya*, Brahman's power, which 'veils man's vision of Brahman, as a result of which man perceives the manifold universe instead of the one Reality'. [177] As a result, *Maya* is often defined as illusion, for although the material world may seem real it is impermanent, being only a temporary manifestation of the power of Brahman. Due to our sense organs, which perceive only this outward manifestation, we tend to regard this as the reality, but this is an illusion, for if we investigate more deeply, through meditation or self-inquiry, we can go beyond *Maya* and discover Brahman, the Ultimate Reality. This accounts for the definition of Advaita Vedanta as nonduality, for in reality no duality exists, there is only Brahman. The Taittiriya Upanishad sums this up beautifully:

> The Lord of Love (Brahman) willed: "Let there be many!"
> He who has no form assumed many forms;
> He who is infinite appeared finite;
> He who is everywhere assumed a place;
> He who is all wisdom caused ignorance;
> He who is real caused unreality.
> It is He who gives reality to all.
> Before the universe was created,
> Brahman existed as unmanifest.
> (Taittiriya Upanishad Part II 6.1-7.1)[178]

Ramakrishna had discovered the veracity of this Vedantic ideal in many of his *sadhanas*, even through his Vaishnavic practices. His discovery that Rama is the transcendental Brahman without form, attributes or name, and that He is all pervasive, pure consciousness, the creator, sustainer and destroyer, is pure Advaita Vedanta. His

---

[177] B. Usha, *A Ramakrishna Vedanta Wordbook*, 1971, Hollywood, p.39
[178] E. Easwaran, *The Upanishads*, 1988, Penguin, New Delhi p.143

realization on achieving *nirvikalpa samadhi* that the Supreme Being when inactive is Brahman the Impersonal God, and also (when active, creating, sustaining and destroying) is *Sakti* (or *Maya*) the Personal God, is a perfect synthesis of Vaishnavism and Advaita Vedanta. To clarify this even further he said,

> The *bhakta* sees that He who is God has also become *Maya*. He Himself has become the universe and all its living beings... Some devotees see everything as Rama...some see everything as Radha and Krishna. [179]

He also describes Brahman in purely Vedantic terms as being eternal, without beginning or end and the nature of Reality: 'the world is illusory and Brahman alone is real. The world is of the nature of magic. The magician alone is real but his magic is unreal.'[180]

Creation

According to Advaita Vedanta creation occurs in cycles, emanating from the One, Brahman, expanding until it reaches a certain point, when it contracts back to a point. Then once again creation occurs, expands and finally contracts back to the One and so on ad infinitum. This occurs 'over an incalculable period of time'[181] and can be likened to a never ending series of big bangs, expansions, contractions and big crunches. The reason for this creation is that Brahman wills it 'because He likes to; because He is free'[182] and its purpose is for His enjoyment

---

[179] The Gospel of Ramakrishna, tr by Sw. Nikhilananda,1942, Ramakrishna-Vivekananda Centre, New York, p.243
[180] *Ibid*, p.585
[181] Sw. Vivekananda, *The Complete Works Vol 2,* 1989, Mayavati, p.239.
[182] Sw. Vivekananda, *The Complete Works Vol 6,* 1989, Mayavati, p.55.

and play. Also the unmanifest Brahman wished to behold Himself and by manifesting into the many He could achieve this:

> All this Creation comes into being
> By the unfoldment of my own power supreme.
> I play with my own *Maya*, My Power Divine.
> The One, I become the many to behold
> My own Form. [183]

As we have seen, Ramakrishna believed in cyclic creation carried out by the power of Brahman, the Divine Mother. He also believed that the creation was the play of Brahman: 'The Divine Mother is always playful and sportive. The universe is her play. ... She wants to continue playing with her created beings. ... Her pleasure is in continuing the game.' [184]

The Nature of Man

Advaita Vedanta regards man as a physical organism through which Brahman senses, experiences and enjoys the world. The essential nature of man, the *atman*, is Brahman, as is everything in creation. However, Brahman needs physical senses to experience his creation and minds to evaluate and enjoy these experiences. The Kena Upanishad says that Brahman is the agent by which the mind thinks, the eyes see, the ears hear, the tongue speaks and the body breathes. (Ch.1 v.5-9)[185] The Katha Upanishad gives the simile of a chariot, of which the *atman* is the master, the body the chariot, the mind the

---

[183] Sw. Vivekananda, *The Complete Works Vol 4,* 1989, Mayavati, p.516.
[184] The Gospel of Ramakrishna, tr by Sw. Nikhilananda,1942, Ramakrishna-Vivekananda Centre, New York, p.136
[185] Sw. Prabhavananda, *The Upanishads*, 1986, Mylapore, p.9

charioteer, the sense organs the horses and the roads travelled on are the objects of sensation. Thus the *atman* is the enjoyer and experiencer of the ride which is made possible by the chariot, charioteer and the horses. (Ch.3 v.3-4)[186] Man overlooks his true nature when he identifies with the mind and body and is oblivious to his true essence, the *atman*. This is picturesquely expressed by the following kirtan sung by Ramakrishna and his devotees:

> O Mother what a machine (the human body) Thou hast made!
> What pranks Thou playest with this toy,
> Three and a half cubits high!
> Holding Thyself within, Thou holdest the guiding strings;
> But the machine, not knowing it,
> Still believes it moves by itself.
> Whoever finds the Mother remains a machine no more.[187]

Ramakrishna said that the ego (I) and the sense of ownership (mine) were the causes of ignorance and that by reasoning and discrimination one could discover that one is the *atman*, free from all attributes. He also described his 'I', in this case the body and mind, as the machine whilst God is its operator, as the house whilst God is the indweller and as the engine whilst God is the engineer. In fact one of his favourite sayings was: 'O Mother I am the machine and Thou art the operator', and this occurs many times throughout *The Gospel of Ramakrishna*.[188]

The Purpose of Life

---

[186] *Ibid*, p.28-29
[187] The Gospel of Ramakrishna, tr by Sw. Nikhilananda,1942, Ramakrishna-Vivekananda Centre, New York, p.193
[188] *Ibid*, p.208-209

According to Advaita Vedanta the purpose or goal of human life is to achieve *moksha* (freedom) by realizing that, in essence, one is the *atman* which is one with Brahman. As Swami Vivekananda, Ramakrishna's most celebrated disciple, said, 'the infinite human soul can never be satisfied but by the infinite itself'.[189] There seems to be a dichotomy between this and the function of a human being as an instrument through which Brahman can experience and enjoy His creation. However, as long as one misidentifies and regards oneself as the ego (mind), then all of one's experiences are filtered through the mind's petty opinions, judgements, preferences, self-interest and worldly concerns. In this case one ceases to be a pure instrument, for all of one's experiences appear as if seen through coloured glass, or the distorting lens of the mind. The only way to be a perfect instrument is to realize one's true essence, resulting in seeing things clearly and as they are. This is because they are seen through a still mind which does not put any particular spin on them. In this case all of one's experiences and sensations are experienced in their immediacy and totality and not corrupted by the mind's narrow concerns. Thus to become a clear instrument of Brahman one needs to achieve the purpose of life, which is to become self-realized.

As can be seen by Ramakrishna's life, he devoted himself to this purpose, that of achieving self-realization, or God-realization, in as many ways as possible. This was done out of his own love of God and spiritual practice, but also so that he could help as many people as possible to fulfil life's purpose on their own particular spiritual path. He

---

[189] Sw.Vivekananda, *The Complete Works Vol 4,* 1989, Mayavati, p.240.

used to say, 'The goal of life is to realize God'[190] and this God-realization is the same as self-realization, for the *atman* and Brahman are one and the same.

The Afterlife

Advaita Vedanta teaches that the *atman* is immortal and, on the death of the human body, is either reabsorbed back into Brahman or is reincarnated. For the *atman* that has attained self-realization there is no rebirth. However, for the *atman* in bondage, that is to say identified with the mind/body, reincarnation occurs so that 'one may gain experience and knowledge and achieve liberation'.[191] As the Katha Upanishad says,

> He who lacks discrimination, whose mind is unsteady and whose heart is impure, is born again and again. But he who has discrimination, whose mind is steady and whose heart is pure, reaches the goal and having reached it is born no more.[192]

As has been previously discussed, Ramakrishna believed in reincarnation for those who have not attained God self-realization. In answer to a question on this, he gave the analogy of a potter and his clay. Potters sell their fired pots, but any that are damaged or imperfect are not fired; instead the clay in them is recycled to make other pots. Similarly 'the Potter (God) won't let you go as long as you are unbaked ... you will be liberated only when you are baked (realize God). Only then will the Potter let you go.'[193] He went on to say that, after self-realization, one goes beyond *Maya* and is no longer reborn.

---

[190] Sw. Chetanananda, *Ramakrishna As We Saw Him*, 1990, St. Louis, p.109
[191] Sw. Ranganathananda, *The Message of the Upanishads*, 1985, Bombay, p.134.
[192] Sw. Prabhavananda, *The Upanishads*, 1986, Mylapore, p.29

Ramakrishna Practices Islam and Christianity

This section will necessarily be in a different format to the previous two, because much less is known about Ramakrishna's views on Islam and Christianity. The reason for this is that they were practised before The Gospel was written and are hardly mentioned in it. This is because, although Ramakrishna's immersion in Hinduism continued throughout The Gospel, he seemed to have conducted his *sadhanas* in Islam and Christianity in comparatively watertight compartments. That is to say, he became interested in them and pursued this interest until he reached, what appeared to him, to be the culmination of each path, after which resumed his Hindu practices. So this section discusses each *sadhana* in turn, but will only be able to carry out a brief comparison between the five elements of world-view, undertaken in the previous sections.

Ramakrishna was exposed to Islam from a very early age, for there were a number of Muslims living in the region of Karmakupur. Once when a child, he and his mother visited the sacred tomb of a Muslim saint on their way to his maternal uncle's home. Whilst at the tomb Gadadhar went into an ecstatic state and sat quietly in this state for some time. Then when he was nine he went to a nearby village to witness the *Namaz*, the recitation of the prayers that are offered five times a day by devout Muslims. This resulted in him having a divine

---

[193] The Gospel of Ramakrishna, tr by Sw. Nikhilananda, 1942, Ramakrishna-Vivekananda Centre, New York, p.669

vision and losing external consciousness, a state in which he remained for two and a half hours.[194] When he was thirty, shortly after his extended practices of Advaita Vedanta, a Sufi mystic Govinda Rai (Wajed Ali Khan) arrived at Dakshineswar temple. There he remained for some time absorbed in prayer and meditation. Ramakrishna was greatly attracted to him, being charmed by his sincere love of and faith in Allah. This resulted in Ramakrishna becoming fascinated by the idea of practicing Islam himself, for he loved to try as many approaches to God as he could and thus verify their validity. About this he said:

> Do you know my attitude? I love all preparations of fish (approaches to God)... I feel myself at home with every dish – fried fish, fish cooked with turmeric, pickled fish; and further, I equally relish rich preparations like fish-head, kalia and pilau.[195]

So he asked Govinda Rai to initiate him into Islam, to which he gladly agreed. Ramakrishna then set about to practice Islam in earnest, moving into a small bungalow from which he had removed all pictures of Hindu deities, eating food prepared under the direction of Muslim (including forbidden food such as onions), dressing like a Muslim, repeating the name of Allah continuously and saying the *Namaz* thrice daily. This last item is the Sufi practice whereas orthodox Muslims offer *Namaz* five times a day.[196] About this he said that during this time he had no desire to see Hindu deities and that his mind completely lost the Hindu way of thinking until after three days lost in this Muslim mood and practice he 'had the full realization of the result of practices according to that faith'.[197] First he had a vision of an effulgent being

---

[194] Sw. Prabhananda, *More About Ramakrishna*, 1993, Calcutta, p.94-95
[195] *Ibid*, p.83
[196] *Ibid*, p.87
[197] Sw. Saradananda, *Sri Ramakrishna The Great Master*, 1978, Mylapore, p.300

with a long beard, then he went into *savikalpa samadhi*, the highest state of communion with Brahman endowed with attributes, and finally he merged into *nirvikalpa samadhi*, union with the attributeless Brahman.

Ramakrishna concluded that the vision was that of Muhammad and, further, that he was a prophet and not an incarnation. This is because the vision did not merge with him, as did the visions of the Hindu Gods, Goddesses and incarnations that he had encountered. This is naturally in complete accord with Islam which believes that Muhammad was a prophet and does not believe in incarnations, for Allah 'has no partners' (Qur'an 6 v.163).[198] The second stage, that of *savikalpa samadhi*, refers to Ramakrishna experiencing Allah as the personal yet formless, God with attributes, which is how the majority of Muslims worship God. The final stage, complete absorption into the formless, attributeless God, is the culmination of many Sufi practices. These stages combine two of the three aspects of divinity: the personal God with form, the personal God without form and the Impersonal Absolute. It is interesting to compare these aspects with Christian Trinity: Jesus, the Holy Ghost and The Father. This experience completely convinced Ramakrishna of the validity of Islam, through which one can approach the divine in both formless aspects, but not that of the personal God with form, as Allah 'has no partners'.[199]

In contrast to Islam, Ramakrishna had no exposure to Christianity as a child. He first came into contact with this religion when he and

---

[198] *'The Koran 7.5'*, Trans by Samir Alicehajic, www.AgnateMoslem.net
[199] Sw. Prabhananda, *More About Ramakrishna*, 1993, Calcutta, p.92-93

Mathurmohan, the son-in-law of Rani Rasmani, visited a Wesleyan Methodist Church and watched the communion service from outside. Mathurmohan had been a devotee of Ramakrishna and had supplied him, at the behest of Rani Rasmani, with all of his daily requirements. On his death in 1871, this function was taken over by Sambucharan ("Sambu") Mallick, who was a great admirer of Christ. Ramakrishna went to visit him regularly and learnt of the life and purity of Jesus for whom he soon developed a great love and regard.[200]

Sambu used to read the Bible to Ramakrishna whenever he visited and it was not long before Ramakrishna desired to practice Christianity. Shortly afterwards this came about spontaneously when he was alone in the house of Jadunath Mallick which was near to Dakshineswar. Ramakrishna often used to go there for a short walk and would be invited inside to rest, even if the master was not at home. One day he was sitting alone in the parlour looking intently at a picture of Jesus sitting in Mary's lap when 'he felt that the picture came to life and that effulgent rays of light, coming out of the bodies of the mother and the child, entered into his heart and changed radically all the ideas of his mind'.[201] He was completely submerged in reverence for and faith in Jesus which completely obliterated his love of the Hindu deities and incarnations, pushing all of his Hindu conditioning to the outer reaches of his mind. He had visions of Christian worshippers offering incense and praying to Jesus, which filled his mind with longing for Him.

---

[200] *Ibid*, p.115-116
[201] Sw. Saradananda, *Sri Ramakrishna The Great Master*, 1978, Mylapore, p.338

On his return to Dakshineswar he remained absorbed in this longing for and meditation on Christ for three days. During this time he completely forgot his priestly duties and did not visit the Kali temple once. On the evening of the third day, whilst in this mood, he saw a man of fair complexion, luminous appearance, with long brilliant eyes and a flat-tipped nose, approaching him. Ramakrishna, charmed by his divine expression, wondered who this could be and as he grew nearer he heard from his own heart the words: 'Jesus The Christ! The great yogi, the loving Son of God, one with the Father, who gave his heart's blood and put up with endless torture, in order to deliver man from sorrow and misery'. [202] The figure then embraced him and merged into him. Ramakrishna then experienced *bhava-samadhi*, a state of ecstasy in which a trace of ego remains, enabling one to enjoy the presence of God. He then lost outer consciousness entering *savikalpa samadhi*, in which one is united with the Absolute with attributes.

From this experience Ramakrishna concluded that Christianity is a valid unique path to God. However, he stressed that contrary to Christian dogma, this is not the only path. He also concluded that Christ was an incarnation, for his vision had merged with Ramakrishna, as had those of previous incarnations he had encountered. Moreover, this does not mean that Christ is the only incarnation, but that he is 'one and the same. Having plunged into the ocean of life, the one God rises up at one point and is known as Krishna; and when after another plunge He rises at another point, He is known as Christ'.[203]

---

[202] *Ibid*, p. 339
[203] Sw. Prabhananda, *More About Ramakrishna*, 1993, Calcutta, p.122

What follows is a short comparison of Ramakrishna's world-view and that of Islam and Christianity; once again using the five elements previously considered.

God

Islam considers God (Allah) to be personal and formless, or formless with attributes. Christianity agrees with this but also believes in the one incarnation. Ramakrishna would have had no problem with either of these concepts, as he experienced both of these aspects of the Absolute or Godhead on many occasions including during his Islamic and Christian *sadhanas*. Sufis also believe in the formless God without attributes, which Ramakrishna experienced many times, one of which was as the culmination of his Islamic and Sufi practices.

Creation

With regard to creation, Ramakrishna would have agreed with both Islam and Christianity that God is the creator and that creation comes from God, but he would have disagreed about the method and nature of creation. For he believed in cyclical creation and that creation is an actual manifestation of God or Brahman, whereas Islam and Christianity believe in a single creation which is basically separate from God; that is, He may be immanent, but everything in creation is not God in manifestation. However, there are Sufis who do not separate God from His creation, for instance Jili who likened the universe to ice and God to the water in which the ice exists; so that although it may appear that forms and the Absolute are different, 'we mystics know they are the same'.[204]

The Nature of Man

Ramakrishna did not believe in resurrection or in the idea of separate eternal souls. He believed that the essence of man, the *atman*, is essentially the same as Brahman and will eventually merge back into this. His views do resonate with Sufism which reveals that it is possible to achieve union with and merge back into, the Godhead.

The Purpose of Life

For Ramakrishna the purpose of life was to realize God and that this included loving God, obeying God and loving and helping one's fellow man. He regarded each person as God in essence and he often used to say that one should treat each jiva (person) as Shiva (God). This agrees with the Christian purpose of loving God and one's neighbour as one's self. The idea of becoming pure, to aid God-realization, also resonates with the Christian idea of becoming perfect so as to enter God's Kingdom. His ideas are also basically in agreement with the Muslim ideal of submission to God (Allah) and 'doing good and spreading goodness on earth'[205]. The Sufis believe that the main purpose of life is to realize God by achieving *fana* (loss of self) so that

---

[204] R.A. Nicholson, *Studies in Islamic Mysticism*, Cambridge, 1921 p.99.
[205] Ziauddin Sardar, *What Muslims Believe,* London, 2006, p.42.

one may achieve union with Him; and wiht this, Ramakrishna is in complete accord.

The Afterlife

The only element where there is almost total disagreement is: what happens after death and what is the nature of the afterlife? For Ramakrishna did not believe in the day of judgement, resurrection, heaven, hell, purgatory, *barzakh*, limbo, or the eternal continuation of souls as separate entities. He believed in reincarnation, unless one is God self-realized, in which case one merges back into Brahman, the Godhead. In this there is some agreement with the Sufis who also hold that it is possible to merge back into the Absolute.

Summing Up

Ramakrishna verified, for him by his own experiences, many diverse Hindu paths, Islam and Christianity. He found that they all lead to at least one of the three aspects of God: the personal in form, the personal without form, the formless with attributes and the formless without attributes. Indeed many of them led to all three, commencing with a vision of God in form, graduating to communion with the formless God with attributes and culminating in complete union with the formless Absolute. Although he did not practice Buddhism, he held the Buddha in high regard, denying that Buddha was an atheist:

> He was not an atheist. He simply could not express his inner experience in words. Do you know what Buddha means? It is to become one with Bodha, Pure Intelligence, by meditating on

> That which is of the nature of pure intelligence; it is to become Pure Intelligence Itself.[206]

Whilst he did not completely agree with the world-view of any particular path, that of Advaita Vedanta and Sufism being nearest to his own views, he had no doubt that all religious paths, if practiced with sincerity and devotion, lead to God-realization. He admitted that all religions contain superstitions and errors, but maintained that this did not matter if the devotee had a deep yearning for God[207] and said that all of the different names that people use for God denote the same Absolute Reality. He decried sectarianism and religious elitism in any form, for as far as he was concerned 'each religion is only a path leading to God, as rivers come from different directions and ultimately become one in the ocean.'[208]

Although followers of particular religions may disagree with this and promote the primacy of their own views, they have not had the breadth of spiritual experience of Ramakrishna. It is indeed fortunate that he was born a Hindu, for Hinduism has not, in general, denied the validity of other religions; although followers of particular Hindu paths have tended to promote their own path as the best, or easiest, way to God-realization. Within this Hindu framework Ramakrishna, who had such love of and yearning for God, plus possessing a deep interest in all spiritual paths, was able to thrive. His view was that God provides different paths to suit the many different temperaments, tendencies

---

[206] The Gospel of Ramakrishna, tr by Sw. Nikhilananda, 1942, Ramakrishna-Vivekananda Centre, New York, p.947
[207] *Ibid*, p.111-112
[208] *Ibid*, p.265

and states of spiritual development, of humanity, and that no path has pre-eminence over any other. About this he said,

> God Himself has provided different forms of worship. He who is the Lord of the Universe has arranged all these forms to suit different men in different stages of knowledge. The mother cooks different dishes to suit the stomachs of her different children. Suppose she has five children. If there is a fish to cook, she prepares various dishes from it — pilau, pickled fish, fried fish and so on — to suit their different tastes and powers of digestion.[209]

The natural corollary to this is that if one believes the purpose of life to be God-realization, one should find the path that one is most suited to, even if this is not the path that one was born into.

---

[209] *Ibid*, p.81

Chapter Seven
Comparison and Conclusion

In comparing the correlation between world-view and self-identity consideration is given to what we are, where we come from and where we go to. For these are the elements of world-view that impinge upon the concept of self-identity most deeply. The remaining elements, the nature of God and the purpose of life, although important, are of lesser concern. The categories used for this comparison are not watertight compartments. Some of the beliefs, teachings, and understandings being considered may fit into more than one category. However, they are a useful device to show the similarities in, and differences between, the various religious paths that are being studied.

The Nature of Man

Firstly considering what we are, there are four main categories: purely material with no eternal essence; containing an essence which will be reinstalled into a resurrected form; containing a soul or spirit which will live on in individual form after death; and containing an essence which will eventually merge back into the Godhead or The Absolute.

Within the first of these categories we find those forms of Orthodox Judaism that do not believe in life after death, and both Theravadan and Tibetan Buddhism. There is an important difference here however, in that the Buddhists believe that the illusory person will be reincarnated again and again until *nirvana* is achieved, when 'the candle will be blown out' and the person will cease to exist, whereas Orthodox Judaism holds that the person will cease to exist upon death.

The second category contains fundamental Christianity and Orthodox Islam, both of which instruct that the person will be resurrected in a body at the Day of Judgement.

In the third category are both Catholic Christians and Gaudiya Vaishnavas, the difference here being that the former believe in only one life before the separation of body and soul occurs, whereas the latter believe in reincarnation, so that this separation occurs many times before becoming final.

In the fourth category we find the Sufis, Advaita Vedantists and followers of the Kabbalah. Once again there are some important differences; the latter two reveal a continual reincarnation and purification until one is fit to be reabsorbed into the Absolute (Brahman or the Ein-Sof); the Sufis aim to achieve that in this lifetime. There is evidence that some Sufis also believe in reincarnation, consider the previously quoted Rumi poem:

> I died as a mineral and became a plant,
> I died as a plant and became an animal,
> I died as an animal and became a man,
> What is there to fear? When have I ever become less by dying?

However, as mainstream Islam and many Sufis do not believe in reincarnation, Rumi's views cannot be considered to apply to Sufism in general.

The Source of Humanity (Where we come from)

In the 'where we come from' class there are three main categories: from dust or physical material, from God or the Absolute and from nothing. The first category contains Orthodox Judaism, both forms of Christianity, Islam and Sufism. This is because these all basically accept the Old Testament in which it is stated quite clearly that man goes from 'dust to dust'. However, they would also all maintain that man's essence, life-force or breath comes from God. This means that their views overflow into the second category, which also contains Advaita Vedanta and Gaudiya Vaishnavism. The difference is that the two Hindu beliefs maintain that not only the essence(or life-force, but also the material universe, are direct manifestations of the divine. Advaita Vedantists understand that All is Brahman, thus everything is a manifestation of Brahman, or pure consciousness, whereas Gaudiya Vaishnavas consider that the universe is a manifestation of Krishna's inferior energy.

This leaves the third category, that of holding that we come from nothing. This could be said to include any religion that teaches creatio ex nihilo – creation out of nothing, which includes Orthodox Judaism and some denominations of Christianity. However, more particularly it includes Kabbalah which states that all creation comes from the Ein-

Sof, the divine nothingness, from which all things come and to which all things return. Both forms of Buddhism also fall into this category, for according to Theravada there is no self, and when this is realized one achieves *nirvana,* entering a domain of nothingness; whereas according to Tibetan Buddhism all is emptiness (*Shunyata*) and nothing intrinsically exists, or has own-existence. In fact it would be more accurate to say that Buddhists reveal that we are 'nothing', so logically we must come from nothing.

One final point, on where we come from: it could be argued that all of the paths that have been studied fall into the second category, that we come from God. This is because Judaism, Christianity and Islam believe that God created the world and everything in it, thus everything in creation comes from God. Also the divine nothingness of Kabbalah is the Godhead, thus Kabbalah also falls into this category. Finally, if one accepts that the greater reality, the nothingness reached after attaining *nirvana,* of Theravadan Buddhism and the Rigpa of Tibetan Buddhism (the luminous emptiness which is the nature of everything) both represent an Absolute Reality, then one could posit that the nothingness which we are, from which we come and to which we return is this Absolute Reality.

The Afterlife

In considering where we go to, there are also three main categories: to nothing, to heaven, hell or purgatory or back into union with God - the Absolute. In the first category we find Orthodox Judaism, those who are not saved in fundamentalist Christianity and both streams of Buddhism, although with differences, as to be expected. Judaism and fundamentalist Christianity believe that we as separate individuals cease to exist and our life-force or breath returns to God; both streams of Buddhism explain that we never had any intrinsic existence and so on achieving *nirvana* we return after death to the nothingness, or emptiness, from which we came.

In the second category we find both streams of Christianity, Islam and Gaudiya Vaishnavism. However, the latter teach a continual reincarnation until Krishna-Loka is achieved, whereas Christianity and Islam both express that one is assigned to heaven, hell or purgatory after death, or at the Day of Judgement. Also Gaudiya Vaishnavas and Catholics both believe that it is the soul or spirit which continues, whereas fundamental Christianity and Islam believe in bodily resurrection.

Finally, in the third category, union with God or The Absolute, we find Sufism, Kabbalah and Advaita Vedanta. As has been previously noted, for Sufis this is, in general, to be attained in one lifetime, whereas for the other two this can take many lifetimes. Also, considering the earlier discussion of the possible Buddhist Absolute Reality, it could be argued that Buddhism fits into this category.

Summing Up

It is interesting to note that Sufism, Kabbalah and Advaita Vedanta all fit into the same categories - coming from God, having an essence which can achieve union with the Godhead and finally merging back into this Godhead. As previously noted it could be posited that this also applies to Buddhism. There are also Christian mystics who have had similar ideas, most notably Dionysius the Areopagite and Meister Eckhart. For Dionysius God was The 'Hidden Dark' and 'The Cause beyond all causes', who 'overflows into all of creation'[210], with whom one could achieve union, becoming 'united, in his better part, to the altogether Unknown'.[211] Meister Eckhart confesses an Absolute Godhead with which we can achieve union and about which he said,

> When I enter the ground, the bottom, the stream and the source of the Godhead, no one asks me where I came from or where I have been. No one missed me there, for there even God [the creator] disappears.[212]

Thus it could be argued that there are mystical streams of all five religions which share the concept of humans as beings that come from, contain an essence of and return to God or The Absolute.

One other topic which has not been systematically studied, but which also affects our world-view and concept of self-identity, is the function of a human being. This has become apparent in many of the paths that have been considered and, whilst linked to the purpose of life, it is not the same thing. For instance, in Advaita Vedanta the function of a human being is as an instrument of Brahman through which He can

---

[210] Michael Cox, *Christian Mysticism*, 1986, London, p.75
[211] *Ibid,* p.76
[212] *Ibid,* p.103

sense, interact with, experience and enjoy the world, whereas the purpose of life is to realize one's unity with Brahman.

This idea of humans as instruments of the divine has been shown in all of the forms of Judaism, Islam and Hinduism which have been studied. In Judaism, as instruments to enjoy and continue the creation; in Islam, as instruments through which Allah could know Himself; in Advaita Vedanta, as instruments through which Brahman could know Himself and His manifestation; and in Gaudiya Vaishnavism, as instruments to perform Yagnas (sacrifices) for the satisfaction of Vishnu. There are also echoes of this in Christianity where man can be seen as an instrument to glorify God and receive His benefits. Tibetan Buddhism also has the concept of the Bodhisattva as an instrument to work for the enlightenment of all beings.

Although the religions studied have many differences, in their views of the world and of self-identity there is one common thread which links them all together - that is the need to transcend the ego, or go beyond one's petty self-interest, concerns, judgements and opinions, so that one can adopt a more universal outlook on life. In Judaism this is necessary so that one can act as an instrument of God in carrying out His dual purpose of enjoyment and creation; and this is to be done by surrendering to His will and obeying His commandments. In Christianity this is necessary so that one can overcome pride by conforming to God's will, thus making one perfect as your Father in heaven is perfect, enabling one to be saved. In Islam this is to be done by total surrender to Allah, so that one can become a perfect instrument through which the Hidden Treasure might be revealed.

In Hinduism this is to be done by overcoming, through knowledge or devotion, the false misidentification of oneself as the ego, thus allowing for union with, or living forever in a heavenly realm with God or The Absolute. Finally, Buddhism requires this transcending of the ego so that one can realize the truth of *anatta*, 'no self,' or *Shunyata*, emptiness, the full realization of which will lead to *nirvana* or liberation.

One of the aims of this study of the world's five main religions has been to make clear why adherents of different religions tend to adopt different lifestyles. Judaism stresses participation in the world through enjoyment and living creatively within the framework of God's commandments. Christianity also stresses living in the world so that we may receive God's benefits and glorify Him, but also has the other-worldly idea of becoming perfect so that we may enter God's Kingdom. Islam considers worldly life to be important, but is more other-worldly still, insisting that its adherents live in complete surrender to Allah, so that through human beings He might know Himself. The followers of Advaita Vedanta face an interesting paradox, for whilst humans are instruments through which Brahman might sense and enjoy his creation, the aim of life is to realize one's unity with Brahman. This aim is to be achieved before one becomes a pure instrument, for as long as one's experience is filtered through the mind's narrow egoistic concerns, this experience is seen through a cloudy filter. However, living in the world is also important for this is how Brahman senses and enjoys His creation. Gaudiya Vaishnavas are exhorted to live in the world, performing sacrifices for the satisfaction of Vishnu, but also to become self-realized through devotion to Krishna so that they may escape from the wheel of life and death and live forever with their beloved Krishna. Finally, both streams of Buddhism consider the world to be suffering, or unsatisfactory, and thus to be transcended by achieving *nirvana*, although in the case of Mahayana Buddhism one should delay this, whilst helping others to achieve this aim. This explains why Buddhism stresses the path of detachment and spiritual practices, which it posits will lead to enlightenment, *nirvana*.

This book has considered the world-view and concept of self-identity in two streams of each of the world's five major religions. It has also attempted to show the correlation between these two ideas, how they interact with and inform each other. Through this study, the similarities and differences between these concepts of world-view and self-identity in the religious paths considered have become apparent. Although there are many fundamental differences, all of these paths stress going beyond the ego and adopting a more universal outlook of life. It is also interesting to note that each religion has a mystical stream which posits that human beings possess the same origin, essence and destination which is God or Absolute Reality. This is not surprising if one agrees with that mystical genius Sri Ramakrishna who, having traversed many of these paths in a variety of religions,[213] decided that ultimately they led to the same realization.

---

[213] S.Saradanand, *Sri Ramakrishna the Great Master*, 1978, Myalpore, p.106-389

Glossary

Advaita: nonduality.

Anatta: no self.

Anicca: impermanence.

Arhat: one who seeks personal enlightenment so as to attain Nirvana and avoid rebirth.

Atman: Brahman within each individual, that portion of the Absolute in each person.

Avatar: an incarnation of an aspect of the Godhead.

Avidya: spiritual ignorance.

Ayin: the nothingness from which 'everything emerges ... and eventually returns there'.

Bardo: intermediate stages between death and rebirth. Bardo literally means 'suspended in between' and Sogyal Rinpoche divides the whole of existence into four bardos: the 'natural' bardo of this life, the 'painful' bardo of dying, the 'luminous' bardo of Dharmadatta and the 'karmic' bardo of becoming.

Bhavanga: in Theravada, an inactive level of mind which is still present when no mental activity is occurring. This is directly transferred from the dying person, at the moment of death, to the embryo (of its new body) as it experiences its first arising of consciousness and so this bhavanga is the causal link between the two.

Bhumi: spiritual stage on the Bodhisattva Path.

Bodhicitta: awakening or enlightenment.

Bodhisattva: one who seeks full enlightenment so as to aid others to do the same.

Brahman: the all-pervading transcendental Absolute Reality.

Darshan: the blessing or purification felt in the presence of holiness.

Dhamma (Buddhist): duty, following the Buddha's teachings to achieve nirvana.

Dharma (Hindu): duty, the criterion which is used to decide whether an action is right or wrong.

Dharmadatta: the realm of 'the clear light' (Dharmakaya) which one encounters on death.

Dharmakaya: the Absolute Unmanifest Reality that is Aware Nothingness.

Dvaita: dualist school of Vedantic philosophy proposed by Madhva.

Ein-Sof (or En-Sof): the infinite nothingness, the source and final resting place of all things.

Fana: absorption into the Absolute, which al-Junaid of Baghdad interpreted as 'dying to self'.

Hadith: Islamic traditions and guidelines based on anecdotal evidence of the life and sayings of the prophet Muhammad.

Hinayana: the 'small vehicle', a derogatory term coined by the Mahayanists for the path of those who seek personal liberation, the Arhats.

Japa: the practice of repeating one of the names of God.

Jiva: the individual self which houses the Atman, and which undergoes rebirth until self-realization (that atman is Brahman) occurs.

Kabbalah: literally 'received wisdom', a mystical stream of Judaism

Kali: the Divine Mother, creator, preserver and destroyer. Sakti, cosmic energy, consciousness in motion.

Kandhas: the five aggregates (form, feeling, perception, mental fabrications and consciousness) which according to the Buddhists make up a human being.

Karma, Kamma: the merit or demerit accrued by your actions and thoughts which determine your present and future lives.

Krishna: an incarnation of Vishnu, the 'preserver'.

Lila: the divine play or manifestation, consciousness in motion.

Mahayana: the 'great vehicle' capable of carrying many people to liberation as a bodhisattva is one who vows not to enter into the final nirvana until all creatures are liberated.

Mandala: an intricate circular motif symbolizing the universe in Hinduism and Buddhism.

Mara: mind-created demons.

Maya: The power of Brahman, which supports the cosmic illusion of the One appearing as the many.

Moksa: liberation from the wheel of birth and death, self-realization, enlightenment.

Mudra: a symbolic hand gesture, designed to connect external actions with spiritual ideas, used in meditation.

Nama: name.

Namah: salutations (to).

Nirmanakaya: the dimension of ceaseless manifestation, or the compassionate energy of Rigpa.

Nirvana: Buddhist word for moksa, enlightenment, awakening.

Nitya: the Ultimate Reality, the eternal Absolute.

Om: Brahman 'The Impersonal Absolute'; but is also the Logos, The Word, and the Ground of Being, in which all manifestation arises, exists and subsides.

Paramitas: perfections to be attained on the Bodhisattva Path.

Prakriti: the manifestation, nature.

Purusa: the witnessing consciousness, or awareness, according to Samkhya unique to each individual.

Rigpa: pure awareness which is 'the nature of everything'.

Sadhana: spiritual practice.

Sakti: cosmic energy, consciousness in motion.

Sambhogakaya: 'the dimension of complete enjoyment' between Dharmakaya and Nirmankya, or 'the radiant luminous nature' of Rigpa.

Samkhya: philosophy proposed by Kapila which posited two fundamental principles, Purusa and Prakriti, as the source of all things.

Samsara: the wheel of birth, life, death and rebirth.

Satchitananda: existence (sat), consciousness (chit), bliss (ananda).

Satsang: association with Truth, normally with a guru or spiritual master.

Sefirot: the stages of divine being and aspects of divine personality.

Siva: universal consciousness when it is at rest, aware of every movement occurring in it, which is 'pure awareness'.

Sunyata: the void, formless awareness, aware nothingness.

Tatagatha: the Buddha.

Talmud: the Jewish book of law.

Tanakh: the Jewish scriptures, also known as The Old Testament.

Theravada: a stream of Buddhism based on the 'Doctrine of the Elders', which is the doctrine of the Buddha that has been preserved and handed down over the centuries by the 'Elders', the senior monks.

Torah: the first five books of the Tanakh.

The Tao: the ultimate principle; the source, which grows and nurtures all things.

Upanishads: the last works of the Vedas, in which ritual was supplanted by the personal and mystical experiencing of the Absolute (Brahman).

Vaishnavism: the worship of Vishnu including that of his Incarnations, Avatars, such as Krishna, Rama etc.

Vedanta: philosophy based on the books at 'the end of the Vedas' i.e. The Upanishads.

Vedas: the most ancient of the Hindu scriptures.

Visishtadvaita-Vedanta: qualified nondualism., which posits that the atman (individual self) is part of the unity of Brahman, but that Brahman has other differentiating qualities above and beyond that of the atman.

Bibliography by Chapters

Judaism Bibliography

Primary Sources:

Internet Sites:
The Bible in Basic English, Speed Bible Software downloaded from www.johnhurt.com

Checked against:

King James Bible, Speed Bible Software downloaded from www.johnhurt.com

Secondary Sources:

Books:
Michael Berg, *The Way*, 2001, John Wiley and Sons, New York
Rabbi Benjamin Blech, *Understanding Judaism*, 1999, Alpha Books, Indianapolis
Dan Cohn-Sherbrook, *Jewish Mysticism*, 1995, One World, Oxford
Rabbi David A Cooper, *God is a Verb*, 1997, Riverhead Books, New York
Carl S. Erlich, *Understanding Judaism*, 2004, Duncan Baird, London
L. E. Goodman, *Jewish Philosophy*, in *The Oxford Companion to Philosophy*, 2005, Oxford Uni Press, Oxford
Rabbi Michael Levin, *Jewish Spirituality and Mysticism*, 2002, Alpha Books, Indianapolis
Eliezer Segal, *Judaism*, in *Life After Death in World Religions*, ed. Harold Coward, 1997, Orbis Books, New York

Christianity Bibliography

Primary Sources:

Internet Sites:
The Bible in Basic English, Speed Bible Software downloaded from www.johnhurt.com

Checked against:

King James Bible, Speed Bible Software downloaded from www.johnhurt.com

Secondary Sources:

Books:
Compact Oxford English Dictionary, 2003, Oxford University Press, Oxford
Louis Berkhof, *A Summary of Christian Doctrine,* London, 1938, The Banner of Truth Trust, London
Michael Cox, *Christian Mysticism,* London, 1986, The Aquarian Press
Anne Geldart, *Christianity,* 1999, Heinemann, Oxford
Duncan Heaster, *Bible Basics,* 2000, The Christadelphian Bible Mission, Birmingham
Thomas Merton, *No Man is an Island,* in *God in All Worlds*, Lucinda Vardey, 1999, Millenium, Alexandria
Joseph Cardinal Ratzinger, *Introduction to Christianity,* 2004, Ignatius Press, San Francisco
John Young, *World Faiths Christianity,* 1006, Hodder and Stoughton, Abingdon

Internet Sites:

Pope John Paul II, *Heaven Hell and Purgatory,*
www.ewtn.com/library/PAPALDOC/JP2HEAVEN.htm#Heaven
Rev William G. Most, *Creation and Angels,*
www.ewtn.com/faith/teachings/goda32.htm
Rev William G. Most, *Christ conquers the Evil of Death,*
www.ewtn.com/faith/teachings/deatha1.htm
Rev William G. Most, *Particular Judgement,*
www.ewtn.com/faith/teachings/judgea1.htm
Rev William G. Most, *The Creation Nature and Fall of Man,*
www.ewtn.com/faith/teachings/goda42.htm
Rev William G. Most, *The Resurrection of the Body,*
www.ewtn.com/faith/teachings/rboda1.htm

Islam Bibliography

Primary Sources:

Internet Sites:
The Koran 7.5, Trans by Samir Alicehajic, downloaded from
www.AgnateMoslem.net

Checked against:

Quran Viewer 1.6, Trans. By Abadullah Yusef Ali, downloaded from www.DivineIslam.com

Secondary Sources:

Books:

Maulana Muhammad Ali, *The Religion of Islam,* 1950, The Ahmadiyyah Anjuman Ishaat Islam, Lahore
John Esposito, *Islam The Straight Path,* 1998, Oxford University Press, Oxford
Shaykh Fadhalla Haeri, *The Thoughtful Guide To Sufism,* 2004, O Books, Alresford (UK)
Masood Ali Khan, *Sufism in Islam,* 2003, Anmol Publications, New Delhi
R.A. Nicholson, *Studies in Islamic Mysticism,* 1921, Cambridge University Press, Cambridge
Martin Lings, *What Is Sufism?,* 1975, George Allen and Unwin, London
Ziauddin Sardar, *What Muslims Believe,* 2006, Granta Books, London
Mohammad Shafii, *Freedom From The Self,* 1985, Human Sciences Press, New York
Colin Turner, *Islam The Basics,* 2006, Routledge, London

Internet Sites:
http:/islam.about.com/od/creation/a/creation.htm
www.islamtomorrow.com/purpose.htm
http:/muslim-canada.org/sufi/sufism.htm
www.nderf.org/islamic_views_nde.htm (Afterlife)
http:/webpages.marshall.edu/~laher1/intro.html

Hinduism Bibliography

Primary Sources:

E. Easwaran, *The Upanishads*, 1988, Penguin, New Delhi
Checked against:
Sw. Prabhavananda, *The Upanishads*, 1968, Ramakrishna Math, Madras

A.C. Bhaktivedanta, *The Bhagavad Gita As It Is*, 1989, The Bhaktivedanta Book Trust, Los Angeles

Secondary Sources:

A.C. Bhaktivedanta, *Dharma*, 1998, The Bhaktivedanta Book Trust, Los Angeles

A.C. Bhaktivedanta, *The Science of Self Realization,* 1977, The Bhaktivedanta Book Trust, Los Angeles
J. Hinnells, *Living Religions,* 1997, Penguin, London
Sw. Nikhilanda, *The Gospel of Ramakrishna,* 1942, Ramakrishna Math, Myalpore
Sw. Ranganathananda, *The Message of the Upanishads*, 1985, Bharatiya Vidya Bhavan, Bombay
H. Rodrigues, *Hinduism,* 2006, Routledge, New York
J. Stillson Judah, *Hare Krishna and the Counterculture,* 1974, John Wiley and Sons, New York
Sw. Saradananda, *Sri Ramakrishna the Great Master*, 1979, Ramakrishna Math, Myalpore
Sw. Vireswarananda, *Srimad Bhagavad-Gita,* 1948, Ramakrishna Math, Madras
Sw. Vivekananda, *The Complete Works Volume 2,* 1989, Advaita Ashram, Mayavati
Sw. Vivekananda, *The Complete Works Volume 4,* 1989, Advaita Ashram, Mayavati
Sw. Vivekananda, *The Complete Works Volume 6,* 1989, Advaita Ashram, Mayavati

Buddhism Bibliography

Books:
Anderson C., *Pain and its Ending*, 1999, Curzon Press, Richmond.
Choong M., *RELS305/405 Buddhism: A History*, 2004, UNE, Armidale
Collins S., *Selfless Persons*, 1982, Cambridge Uni Press, Cambridge
Dalai Lama The, *The World of Tibetan Buddhism,* 1995, Wisdom Publications, Boston
Evans-Wentz W.Y. *The Tibetan Book of Great liberation,* 2000, Oxford University Press, New York
R. Gethin, *The Foundations of Buddhism,* 1998, Oxford Uni Press, Oxford
Easwaran E. *The Dhammapada*, 1986, Nilgiri Press, Petaluma.
Gombrich R.F. *Theravada Buddhism,* 1988, Routledge and Kegan Paul, London
Gowans C., *The Philosophy of the Buddha*, 2003, Routledge, London.
Harvey P., *An Introduction to Buddhism*, 1990, Cambridge Uni Press, Cambridge.
Rinpoche S., *The Tibetan Book of Living and Dying*, 1992, Harper Collins, San Francisco
Trungpa C., *Cutting Through Spiritual Materialism*, 1987, Shambala, Boston
Watts A.W., *The Way of Zen*, 1957, Pantheon Books, New York
Williams P., *Buddhist Thought*, 2000, Routledge, London

Internet Sites:
http://webspace.ship.edu/cgboer/buddhacosmo.html
http://buddhism.kalachakranet.org/resources/purpose_life_dalai_lama.html
www.buddhism.about.com/6/a/2003_12_03
www.religionfacts.com/buddhism/beliefs/purpose.htm

Ramakrishna Bibliography

Primary Source:

Sw. Nikhilanda, *The Gospel of Ramakrishna,* 1942, Ramakrishna Math, Mylapore

Secondary Sources:

Sw. Ananyananda, *Life of Sri Ramakrishna*, 1983, Advaita Ashrama, Mayavati
A.C. Bhaktivedanta, *The Bhagavad Gita As It Is*, 1989, The Bhaktivedanta Book Trust, Los Angeles
A.C. Bhaktivedanta, *Dharma*, 1998, The Bhaktivedanta Book Trust, Los Angeles
Sw. Chetanananda, *Ramakrishna As We Saw Him*, 1990, Vedanta Society of St. Louis, St Louis
E. Easwaran, *The End of Sorrow*, 1983, Blue Mountain Centre of Meditation, Petaluma
E. Easwaran, *The Upanishads*, 1988, Penguin, New Delhi
R.A. Nicholson, *Studies in Islamic Mysticism*, 1921, Cambridge University Press, Cambridge
Sw. Prabhananda, *More About Ramakrishna*, 1993, Advaita Ashram, Calcutta
Sw. Prabhavananda, *The Upanishads*, 1968, Ramakrishna Math, Madras
Sw. Ranganathananda, *The Message of the Upanishads*, 1985, Bharatiya Vidya Bhavan, Bombay
H. Rodrigues, *Hinduism*, 2006, Routledge, New York
Sw. Saradananda, *Sri Ramakrishna the Great Master*, 1979, Ramakrishna Math, Mylapore
Ziauddin Sardar, *What Muslims Believe,* 2006, Granta Books, London
Mohammad Shafii, *Freedom From The Self,* 1985, Human Sciences Press, New York
J. Stillson Judah, *Hare Krishna and the Counterculture,* 1974, John Wiley and Sons, New York
H. Torwesten, *Ramakrishna and Christ*, 1999, The Ramakrishna Mission Institute of Culture, Calcutta
B. Usha, *A Ramakrishna Vedanta Wordbook*, 1971, Vedanta Press
Sw. Vivekananda, *The Complete Works Volume 2,* 1989, Advaita Ashram, Mayavati

Sw. Vivekananda, *The Complete Works Volume 4,* 1989, Advaita Ashram, Mayavati
Sw. Vivekananda, *The Complete Works Volume 6,* 1989, Advaita Ashram, Mayavati

Internet Sites:
The Koran 7.5, Trans by Samir Alicehajic, downloaded from www.AgnateMoslem.net

INDEX

A
Absolute, 37, 41, 88, 115, 118. *see also* Brahman
   and Buddhism, 35, 63
   and Christianity, 23, 24
   and Hinduism, 49, 51, 56, 57, 58, 60, 61, 85, 88, 94, 104
   and Islam, 35, 36
   and Judaism (Torah-based), 10, 11, 12
   and Kabbalah, 12, 15, 21
   Ramakrishna on, 108
   and Sufism, 37, 39–41, 106, 107
Acts *28 v.28*, 23
Adam and Eve, 28
Adhayatma Ramayana, 89
Advaita Vedanta. *see also* Absolute; Brahman; Ramakrishna and Advaita Vedanta; Upanishads
   introduction to, 48
   and afterlife, 57
   and creation, 52
   and function of human being, 115
   and Gaudiya Vaishnavism, compared, 59–61
   and nature of man, 54–55
afterlife
   and Buddhism, 68–69, 72–74
   and Christianity, 30–32
   and Hinduism, 57–59
   and Islam, 43–44
   and Judaism (Torah-based), 17–18
   and Ramakrishna, 92, 93, 99–100, 107
   and Sufism, 45
   and Vaishnavism, 92–93
   summary of views, 110–111, 113–114
Against Heresies, 26
Aitareya Upanishad, 49
   3 v.1, 50
Allah, 35–37, 44, 45, 46, 47, 102–103. *see also* Islam; Qur'an; Sufism
Ananyananda, Swami, 88
anatta, 68, 69, 70, 72, 75
anicca, 70, 75
annihilationism, 63
anthropomorphism and Judaism (Torah-based), 11–12

arhat, 63
atheism and Buddhism, 63
atman, 55, 56, 57, 59–60, 63, 68, 90, 96–99
avatar, 48, 82
awareness, pure, 50, 64. *see also* Absolute

B

baptism, 29
bardos, 73
barzakh, 40, 43
Benedict XVI, Pope, 31
Berg, Michael, 17
Berkhof, Louis, 26, 27
Bhagavad Gita, 55, 88
   2 v.13, 58
   3 v.9, 54
   8 v.20, 51
   9 v.18, 51
   9 v.24, 54
   9 v.4, 51
   9 v.5, 51
   9 v.6, 51
   10 v.20-42, 51
   11 v.19, 51
   14 v.15, 59
bhaktas, 89, 91, 95
bhakti and Vaishnavism, 52, 83
Bhaktivedanta, A.C., 49, 51, 54, 55, 56, 57, 59, 88, 90, 91
bhava-samadhi, 104
bhavanga, 72
bhedabheda, 53
Bible, Holy, 23, 26, 103
big bang, 21, 25, 38, 49, 52, 96
big crunch, 21, 49, 52, 96
Big Mind, 64, 65, 66
Blech, Rabbi Benjamin, 13, 21
Bodhidharma, 65
Bodhisattva, 62, 71, 72
Boeree, C. George, 68
Bon religion, 62
Brahman. *see also* Absolute
   aspects of, 81
   and creation, 52, 96
   described, 49–51, 59–61, 89
   and function of human being, 115, 117

Krishna, compared to, 51–52
   and Maya, 94–95
   merging with, 57–58, 84–86, 90
   and nature of man, 54–55, 96–97
   and purpose of life, 56–57, 98–99
Brahmani, 82
breath, as life force, 14–15, 22, 27, 40, 53, 112
Brihadaranyaka Upanishad, 50, 58
Buddha, 70, 73, 108
   bodies of, 67–68
   silence of, 63–64
   and Vedanta, 63
Buddha-Nature, 63
Buddhism, 62–76
   and Absolute, 35, 63
   and afterlife, 68–69, 72–74
   as atheistic, 63
   and creation, 66–68
   and death, 65, 72–73, 75
   and ego, 116
   Eightfold Path, 70
   Four Noble Truths, 67, 70
   and function of human being, 116
   Hinayana, 62–63
   and lifestyles, 117
   and light, 65, 74–75
   and love, 71
   Mahayana, 62, 67, 69, 71, 76, 117
   and nature of man, 68–70
   and purpose of life, 70–72
   and suffering, 64
   Theravadan, 72–73, 75, 110, 112, 113
   Tibetan, 62, 63, 64, 67–68, 69, 73, 75, 110–111, 113, 116
bundle-moments, 68–69

C
Cartesian dualism, 15. *see also* dualism
Catholicism, 6–7, 27, 28–29, 111, 114
   and afterlife, 31–32
   and Christadelphianism, compared, 32–34
   and creation, 26
   grace, gift of, 28
   and heaven, 31

and hell, 31–32
and salvation, 26
Chaitanya, 48, 49, 53, 82
Chandogya Upanishad
   3 v.14.1, 49
   4 v.15, 58
chariot metaphor, 55
Chetanananda, Swami, 99
Choong, Mun-keat, 70
Christ as Krishna, 105
Christ, Jesus, 24. *see also* Christianity, Catholicism, Christadelphianism
   Islamic view of, 35
Christadelphianism
   and afterlife, 30–31
   and Catholicism, compared, 32–34
   and hell, 32
   and purpose of life, 29
Christianity, 23–34
   and Absolute, 23, 24
   and afterlife, 30–32
   and creation, 25–26
   and death, 27–28, 27–28, 30, 30–32
   and ego, 24, 33–34, 116
   and function of human being, 116
   and immanence, 23
   and Islam, compared, 45, 100–107
   and lifestyles, 117
   and light, 24
   and love, 24, 29, 33
   mystical, 114–115
   and Ramakrishna. *see* Ramakrishna and Christianity
   and visions, 103–104
Chronicles *2 v.5*, 10
Clear Light, 65
Cohn-Sherbrook, Dan, 15
Collectio Lacencis, 26
Collins, S., 73
Colossians
   1 v.15, 25
   1 v.16-17, 25
   1 v.20, 26
comparisons among religious streams
   and afterlife, 113–114
   and nature of man, 110–111
   and source of humanity, 112–113

summarized, 114–118
compassion, 62, 71-72
consciousness and Kabbalistic Judaism, 13–14. *see also* Absolute; Brahman; Krishna
Cooper, Rabbi David, 12, 13, 14, 16, 17
2 Corinthians *9 v.8*, 23
covenant, 16
Cox, Michael, 115
creatio ex nihilo, 21
creation, 46
   and Buddhism, 66–68
   and Christianity, 25–26
   as cyclical, 52–53, 95–96
   and Hinduism, 52–54
   and Islam, 37–39
   and Judaism (Torah-based), 12–14
   and Ramakrishna, 105–106
   and Vaishnavism, 88–89
creationism, 27
cyclical creation, 52–53, 95–96

D
Dalai Lama, 63, 69, 70, 71
Daniel
   2 v.47, 10
   9 v.14, 11
dasya, 83
Day of Judgement, 43
death, 110–111. *see also* afterlife
   and Buddhism, 65, 68–69, 72–73, 75
   and Christianity, 27–28, 30–32
   and Hinduism, 57–59, 93, 99
   and Islam, 40, 42, 44, 45
   and Judaism (Torah-based), 15, 20
Deuteronomy
   6 v.4, 10
   8 v.18, 20
   10 v.14, 10
   19 v.1-3, 11
   23 v.14, 11
Devi Purana, 89
devotion, 52, 83
Dhammapada, 72
dharma, 57, 88
Dharmakaya, 67–68

Divine Mother, 81, 85, 86, 89, 96
Doctrine of the Elders, 62
dualism, 15, 19, 32, 40, 48, 51, 61
Dudjon Rinpoche, 64
dukkha, 67, 75

E

Easwaran, Eknath, 50, 88, 92, 94
Ecclesiastes
   3 v.19-20, 18
   5 v.2, 10
Eckhart, Meister, 115
ego, 104
   and Buddhism, 116
   and Christianity, 24, 33–34
   and Hinduism, 55, 60, 90, 97, 98, 104
   and Islam, 45, 46, 47
   and Judaism, 19, 22
   religions compared regarding, 116–117
   and Sufism, 37, 41
Eightfold Path, 70
Ein-Sof, 12, 15, 21
emptiness, 63, 69, 70, 76, 113, 114, 116
enlightenment, 5, 62, 71, 116, 117
Epistle of Light, 41
Erlich, Carl S., 10, 12, 16
Esposito, John, 42
essence, as soul or soul-like, 32, 34, 40, 67-68, 87, 110. *see also* soul; breath
eternalism, 63
Evans-Wentz, W.Y., 67

F

false self. *see* ego
fana, 35, 37, 45. *see also* ego
Father, the, 24
five pillars of Islam, 42, 43. *see also* Islam
Four Noble Truths, 67, 70
function of human being, 115–117

G

Galatians *3 v.2*, 23
Garbodakasayi Vishnu, 53

Gaudiya Vaishnavism, 48, 53, 55, 56, 58, 59, 116
    and Advaita Vedanta, compared, 59–61
Gehenna, 43
Geldart, Anne, 25, 29
Genesis
    1, 11
    1 v.1-41, 12
    1 v.24, 13
    1 v.27, 11, 13
    1 v.3, 13
    1 v.31, 13
    2 v.3, 16
    2 v.7, 14
    3 v.19, 15
    7 v.15, 14
    9 v.7, 20
Gethin, R., 64
gidams, 68
God. see Absolute; Allah; Brahman; Christ; Krishna; various religions
Golden Rule, 16, 22
Goloka-Vrindavan, 58
Gombrich, R.F., 62
Goodman, Leen E., 16
Gospel of Ramakrishna, The, 78, 80, 81, 82, 83, 84, 85, 88, 89, 90, 93, 95, 96, 97, 98, 100, 108, 109
Goswami, Jiva, 48
grace, gift of, 28
Great Commandment, 29
Ground Luminosity, 64, 68, 73, 74
Gupta, Mahendranath, 78

H

Haeri, Shaikh Fadhalla, 43
hajj, 42
Hallaj, 37
Hanuman, 82
happiness, 26, 56, 71, 91, 92
Harvey, P., 62, 64, 65, 67, 69
Heaster, Duncan, 27, 29, 30, 31
heaven, 31–32, 43, 44
Hebrews
    4 v.12-14, 23
    11 v.3, 25
    12 v.29, 24, 34
hell, 31–32, 43, 44

Herschel, Abraham Joshua, 19
Hidden Treasure, 38–39, 47
Hinayana Buddhism, 62–63. *see also* Buddhism
Hinduism, 48–61. *see also* Advaita Vedanta; Vaishnavism
    and Absolute, 49, 51, 56, 57, 58, 60, 61, 85, 88, 94, 104
    and afterlife, 57–59
    avatars, 48
    and creation, 52, 54
    and death, 93, 99
    defined, 48
    and ego, 116
    and lifestyles, 117
    and light, 50, 58
    and love, 52
Hinnells, John R., 48
Holy Bible, 23, 26, 103
Holy Ghost, 24
Holy Trinity, 24

I

illusion, world as, 53–54, 69, 84–85, 94–95
immanence
    and Christianity, 23
    and Islam, 36, 37
    and Judaism (Torah-based), 11, 12, 19
impermanence, 70, 75
infusion, 27
instruments, humans as, 115–117
Irenaeus, Saint, 26
Isaiah
    8 v.8-10, 11
    28 v.26, 11
    50 v.7, 11
    57 v.15, 10
    65 v.17, 31
Isha Upanishad
    v.4, 50
    v.5, 50
    v.8, 50
Islam, 35–47. *see also* Allah; Qur'an; Sufism
    and Absolute, 35, 36
    and afterlife, 43–44
    and Allah, 35–37
    and Christianity, compared, 45, 100–107
    and creation, 37–39

and death, 40–42, 44, 45
and ego, 116
and function of human being, 115–116
and lifestyles, 117
meaning of, 42
and nature of man, 39–41
and purpose of life, 42
and Ramakrishna. *see* Ramakrishna and Islam
and Sufism, compared, 45–47

J

Jatadhari, 83
Jeremiah *3 v.23*, 11
Jili, 37, 39, 106
jiva, 57, 58, 60
Jiva Goswami, 48
Job
   12 v.13, 11
   27 v.3, 11
   36 v.26, 10
1 John
   1 v.18, 23
   1 v.5, 24
   3 v.20, 23
   4 v.12, 23
   4 v.24, 23
   4 v.8, 24
   5 v.4, 23
   5 v.7-10, 24
   5 v.7-9, 23
   14 v.6, 24
   20 v.22, 24
John Paul II, Pope, 31, 32
Joshua *1 v.9*, 11
Judah, J. Stillson, 51, 55, 88, 90, 93
Judaism (Torah-based), 10–22. *see also* Kabbalistic Judaism
   and Absolute, 10, 11, 12
   and afterlife, 17–18
   and anthropomorphism, 11–12
   and creation, 12–14
   and death, 15, 20
   and ego, 22, 116
   and function of human being, 115
   and God, 10–12
   and immanence, 11

and Kabbalistic Judaism, compared, 18–22
and lifestyles, 117
and light, 13
and love, 16, 20
as monotheistic, 10
as polytheistic, 10
and purpose of life, 19–20

K

Kabbalistic Judaism, 12, 15, 21. *see also* Judaism (Torah-based)
and afterlife, 17
and consciousness, 13–14
and creation, 13–14
and Ein-Sof, 12, 15, 21
and free will, 14
and Judaism (Torah-based) compared, 18–22
and soul, 14–16, 19
Kali, 81, 86
kandhas, 68, 75
Karanodakasayi Vishnu, 53
karma, 58, 59, 68, 69, 72, 74, 75, 92
Katha Upanishad, 99
   I v.1, 56
   2 v.18, 50
   3 v.15, 50
   3 v.3-4, 55
   3 v.3-4, 97
Kena Upanishad
   1 v.1-9, 54
   1 v.2, 50
   1 v.3, 50
   1 v.5-9, 50, 97
   2 v.5, 56
Koran. *see* Qur'an
Krishanloka, 58, 59
Krishna
   abode of, 58
   and afterlife, 59
   attitude toward, 83
   Brahman, compared to, 51–52
   as Christ, 105
   as creator, 53–54
   devotion to, 55
   and God, 105
   qualities of, 51–52

and Ramakrishna, 84, 87–90, 92–93
    surrender to, 56–57
    and Vaishnavism, 49, 60–61
Krishna Consciousness, 57, 59
Krishnaloka, 60, 92
Kshirodakasayi, 53
Kundalini, 82–83

L

Levin, Rabbi Michael, 14, 18
Leviticus
    19 v.18, 16
    25 v.42, 19
liberation, 54. *see also* enlightenment; *nirvana*; self-realization
life force, as breath, 14–15, 22, 27, 40, 53, 112
life, purpose of. *see* purpose of life
lifestyles, religions compared regarding, 117
light
    and Buddhism, 65, 74–75
    and Christianity, 24
    and Hinduism, 50, 58
    and Judaism (Torah-based), 13
    and Kabbalistic Judaism, 12, 13–14, 17, 20
    and Ramakrishna, experience of, 79, 103
Lings, Martin, 38
love
    and Buddhism, 71
    and Christianity, 24, 29, 33
    and Hinduism, 52
    and Islam, 47
    and Judaism (Torah-based), 16, 20
    and Ramakrishna, 83, 84, 86, 94, 109
    and Sufism, 37, 43
Luke
    12 v.10, 24
    17 v.21, 23
luminous emptiness, 75

M

madhur, 83, 84
magic, world as, 95
Mahayana Buddhism, 62, 67, 69, 71, 76, 117. *see also* Buddhism

Mallick, Jadunath, 103
Mallick, Sambucharan, 103
mandala, 68
mantra, 68
Mark *12 v.29*, 23
Matthew
   5 v.48, 30, 34
   6 v.10, 30
   11 v.29, 34
   16 v.24-26, 33
   22 v.37-38, 29
   28 v.18-20, 24
maya, 53–54, 69, 84–85, 94–95
Mecca, 42
meditation, 68, 94
Merton, Thomas, 30
moksha, 98
monism, 18
monotheism, 10
Most, William G., 26, 28, 31
mudra, 68
Muhammad, 102
Muhammad Ali, Maulana, 40
mukti, 54
Mundaka Upanishad, 50, 56
mysticism, 114–115, 118. *see also* Kabbalalistic Judaism; Sufism

N

nafs, 40. *see also* breath, as life force
Nagarjuna, 67
Namaz, 101
Nasafi, 45
nature of man
   and Buddhism, 68–70
   and Christianity, 27–28
   and Hinduism, 54–56, 96–97
   and Islam, 39–41
   and Judaism (Torah-based), 14–16
   summary of views, 110–111
   and Vaishnavism, 90–91
Nicholson, R.A., 37, 106
Nirmanakaya, 67–68
nirvana, 62, 63, 64, 67, 68, 71, 72, 74–76, 111, 112, 117
nirvikalpa samadhi, 85, 86, 90, 95
no-self, 68, 69, 70, 72, 75

nondualism. see Advaita Vedanta
nothingness, 74
Numbers *23 v.19*, 11
Nursi, Said, 41

P
Padmasambhava, 62, 64, 74
paramatman, 51, 53, 55, 60, 90, 91
Parousia, 30
1 Peter 5 v.5, 23
2 Peter *1 v.4*, 29, 34
pitr-loka, 58
polytheism, and Judaism (Torah-based), 10
potter and clay, analogy of, 99–100
Prabhananda, Swami, 103, 105
Prabhavananda, Swami, 99
Prabhupada, A.C.Bhaktivedanta Swami, 8. see Bhaktivedanta
prajnaparamita, 63
Prasna Upanishad, 56
pre-existentialism, 27
Proverbs *30 v.5*, 11
Psalms
   7 v.11, 11
   47 v.7, 11
   62 v.8, 11
   68 v.20, 11
   75 v.7, 11
   99 v.9, 10
purpose of life
   and Buddhism, 70–72
   and Christadelphianism, 29
   and Christianity, 28–30
   compared to function, 115
   and Hinduism, 56–57, 98–99
   and Islam, 42
   and Judaism (Torah-based), 16
   and Kabbalistic Judaism, 17
   Ramakrishna, according to, 106–107
   and Sufism, 42–43
   and Vaishnavism, 91–92

Q
Qur'an. *see also* Allah; Islam; Sufism
   1 v.122, 36
   1 v.131, 36

1 v.171, 35
1 v.34, 37
1 v.45, 36
2 v.105, 36
2 v.109, 36
2 v.163, 36
2 v.173, 36
2 v.181, 36
2 v.211, 36
2 v.251, 36
2 v.257, 36
2 v.268, 36
2 v.30, 42
2 v.94, 44
2 v.96, 36
2 v.98, 37
3 v.14, 44
3 v.182, 36
3 v.19, 36
3 v.4, 36
3 v.51, 37
3 v.55, 43
3 v.97, 36
4 v.134, 44
5 v.17, 35
5 v.17-18, 36
5 v.72, 35
51 v.56-58, 42
6 v.163, 102
6 v.35-36, 44
6 v.37, 36
67 v.35, 36
7 v.54, 38
8 v.24, 36
8 v.46, 36
8 v.62, 36
13 v.16, 36
19 v.30, 44
20 v.73, 36
21 v.30, 38
21 v.35, 36, 40
22 v.16, 36
23 v.101-108, 43
23 v.104, 44
29 v.57, 40

30 v.9, 37
31 v.30, 36
37 v.163, 44
37 v.43-49, 44
45 v.29-30, 44

R

Radha, 84
Rai, Govinda, 101
Rajneesh, S., 65
Rama, 82, 83–84, 87, 88, 95
Ramakrishna, 77–109, 118
    and Absolute, 108
    and afterlife, 107
    as avatar, 82
    biography, 79–86
    childhood, 80
    and Christianity, 100–107, 102–105
    on creation, 105–106
    and cyclical creation, 96
    and Divine Mother, 81, 85
    and Hanuman, 82
    his approach compared to others, 91–92
    Islam compared to Christianity, 100–107
    and Kali, worship of, 81, 86
    and Kundalini, 82–83
    and light, 79, 103
    and love, 83, 84, 86, 94, 109
    as mother, 83–84
    and nirvikalpa samadhi, 85, 86
    parents of, 79
    and purpose of life, 106–107
    and *samadhi*, 86
    summary of views, 107–109
    and Tantra, 82–83
    visions, Christian, 103–104
    as woman, 84
Ramakrishna and Advaita Vedanta, 84–86, 93–100
    and afterlife, 99–100
    and creation, 95–96
    and God, nature of, 94–95
    and nature of man, 96–98
    and purpose of life, 98–99
Ramakrishna and Islam, 100–107
    Allah, 102–103

    exposure to, 100–101
    Muhammad, insights into, 102
Ramakrishna and Vaishnavism, 87–93
    and afterlife, 92–93
    and cyclical creation, 88–89
    and purpose of life, 91–92
Ramkumar, 81
Ramlala, 83–84
Ranganathananda, Swami, 57, 99
Rasmani, Rani, 80, 103
reincarnation. *see* afterlife
religions
    introduction to, 4–9
    summary of views, 114–118
resurrection, 40, 43, 44, 45
Revelations
    15 v.1, 23
    3 v.12, 29
rigpa, 64, 65, 68
Rodrigues, Hillary, 92
Romans
    1 v.9, 23
    2 v.2, 23
    11 v.22, 23
Rumi, 40, 111

S

sadhana, 77
sakhya, 83
Sakti, 81, 95
salvation and Catholicism, 26
samadhi, 86
Sambhogakaya, 67–68
samsara, 63, 66–67, 72, 74, 75, 76
2 Samuel *14 v.20*, 10
Sankhya, 51
santa, 83
Saradananda, Swami, 102, 103, 118
Sardar, Ziauddin, 42, 107
savikalpa samadhi, 91, 102, 104
Sefirot, 12, 15
Segal, Eliezer, 15, 17
Self, 65. *see also* Brahman
self-identity. *see* nature of man
self-inquiry, 94

145

self-realization, 57, 60, 98–99
separateness. *see* ego
Shafii, Muhammad, 35, 40
Shiva, 81
shunyata , 67, 69, 76. *see also* emptiness
singularity, 49
Sita, 82
Siva, 53
Sogyal Rinpoche, 64, 65, 67, 68, 71, 73, 74
soul, 40, 58, 60
   and Christianity, 27, 28, 32, 33, 34
   and Judaism (Torah-based), 14–15, 19
   and Kabbalistic Judaism, 14-16
source of humanity, views summarized, 111–113
spirit, 40
Srimad Bhagavatam, 1.2.11, 51, 56, 91
string theory, 69
substratum, 50
suffering, 64, 67, 70, 72, 75
Sufism, 35, 37, 39. *see also* Allah; Islam; Qur'an
   and Absolute, 37, 39, 41, 106, 107
   and afterlife, 45
   and Allah, 37
   and Islam compared, 45–47
   and love, 37, 43
   and nature of man, 39–41
   and purpose of life, 42–43
supreme planet, 58
surrender, 43, 56, 57
Suzuki, Shunryu, 66
Svetasvetara Upanishad
   6 v.10-12, 55
   3 v.1, 50
   2 v.14, 56

T
Taittiriya Upanishad *Part II 6.1-7.1*, 52, 94
Talmud, 13
Tantra, 82–83
Tathagata, 65
Theravadan Buddhism, 72–73, 75, 110, 112, 113. *see also* Buddhism
Tibetan Book of the Dead, The, 65, 75
Tibetan Buddhism, 62, 63, 64, 67, 67–68, 69, 73, 75, 110–111, 113, 116. *see also* Buddhism
1 Timothy *2 v.4*, 28

Torah. see Judaism (Torah-based)
Torwesten, Hans, 89
Totapuri, 84–86
Traducianism, 27
Tri-Kaya, 67
Trinity, Holy, 24
Trungpa, Chogyam, 71
Turner, Colin, 38, 40, 41

U
Ultimate Reality. see Absolute; Brahman
Universal Mind, 64, 65, 66
Unterman, A., 12, 14
Upanishads. See Aitareya; Brihadaranyaka; Chandogya; Isha; Katha; Kena; Mundaka; Prasna; Svetasvetara; Taittiriya
Usha, Brahmacharini, 85, 87, 91, 94

V
va-omerelohim (And God said), 12
Vaishnavism, 8, 48, 51, 79, 83. *see also* Ramakrishna and Vaishnavism
    and afterlife, 92–93
    bhakti and, 52
    creation, view of, 88–89
    God, view of, 87–88
    nature of man, view of, 90–91
    and purpose of life, 91–92
    and Ramakrishna, 87–93
vatsalya, 83
Vedanta and Buddha, 63. *see also* Advaita Vedanta
Vishnu, 48, 53, 54, 55, 79, 87, 90
visions, Christian, 103–104
Vivekananda, Swami, 56, 58, 96, 98

W
Williams, Paul, 7, 67, 69, 73

Y
yagnas, 54
Yoga, 51
youmm, 38
Young, John, 32

Z
Zen, 65

Zen Mind, Beginner's Mind, 66
Zohar. *see* Kabbalistic Judaism

About Colin Drake...

I was born in London in 1948 and, after a happy childhood, attended Kent College in Canterbury from 1959-65. I then took a degree in mathematics at London University before gaining a job as a trainee computer programmer and working on large mainframe computers until 1972, when during a visit to East Africa I met Janet who was to become my life-long partner. After some time living in London together and travelling to Canada and the USA, we came to live in Australia, which was Janet's homeland. We lived worked and studied in Sydney for seven years before buying an old run-down macadamia farm in the mountain range on the NSW/QLD border where we established a pottery, Janet having qualified as a studio production potter. Here we have lived happily ever since, having two fine sons who have now left home, and being deeply involved in yoga and spiritual life. Janet is now a qualified yoga teacher and I have recently completed an honours degree in comparative religion and philosophy.

This book, *Humanity: Our Place in The Universe,* is a direct outcome of my honours year at The University of New England, comprising my thesis and coursework essay on Ramakrishna, who was chosen to highlight the themes examined in the thesis. This is, to my knowledge, the only book published that directly examines the central beliefs of the world's religions within the same framework, which allows for straightforward comparison of these beliefs.

I have also completed another book entitled *Beyond the Separate Self, The End of Anxiety and Mental Suffering* which is a 'simple guide to awakening' based upon over 40 years of spiritual search, practice and experiences. This book contains meditations/contemplations written over a twelve year period since my first 'awakening' in 1996, and also contains relevant essays from my university days which have been modified to highlight the themes explored in this book.

www.ingramcontent.com/pod-product-compliance
Lightning Source LLC
Chambersburg PA
CBHW032124090426
42743CB00007B/454